P9-DNK-592

The Ultimate
Candy Book

The Ultimate

. . . .

Also by Bruce Weinstein

The Ultimate Ice Cream Book
The Ultimate Party Drink Book

Candy Book

MORE THAN 700 QUICK AND EASY, SOFT AND
CHEWY, HARD AND CRUNCHY SWEETS AND TREATS

BRUCE WEINSTEIN

WILLIAM MORROW
An Imprint of HarperCollinsPublishers

In memory of my grandpa, Joe Helfman

"Sugar sugar sugar please"

THE ULTIMATE CANDY BOOK. Copyright © 2000 by Bruce Weinstein. All rights reserved. Printed in the United States of America. No part of this book may be used or reproduced in any manner whatsoever without written permission except in the case of brief quotations embodied in critical articles and reviews. For information address HarperCollins Publishers Inc., 10 East 53rd Street, New York, NY 10022.

HarperCollins books may be purchased for educational, business, or sales promotional use. For information please write: Special Markets Department, HarperCollins Publishers Inc., 10 East 53rd Street, New York, NY 10022.

FIRST EDITION

Designed by Mary Austin Speaker

Illustrations by Alexis Seabrook

Library of Congress Cataloging-in-Publication Data

Weinstein, Bruce, 1960–
   The ultimate candy book : more than 700 quick and easy, soft and chewy, hard and crunchy sweets and treats / by Bruce Weinstein.—1st ed.
      p.   cm.
   ISBN 0-688-17510-4
   1. Candy.   I. Title.
   TX791 .W382 2000
   641.8'53—dc21   00–032863

        03   04 /QW   10   9   8   7   6

CONTENTS

ACKNOWLEDGMENTS

IT WAS MY JOY and good fortune to work with the talented and professional team that made this book happen, including:

Harriet Bell, my editor and newfound friend. I can't thank her enough for standing behind this book from day one and pushing me through it with incredible wisdom, good humor, and honesty.

Editorial assistant Karen Ferries. She always had a smile no matter how many times I called or how many questions I asked.

Susan Ginsburg, my agent, lunch buddy, phone and e-mail pal (and Annie Leuenberger, her tireless and incredibly organized assistant at Writers House). I've always felt that I was in good hands, and never more so than I do right now.

Mary Ellen Bartley, photographer extraordinaire. Her photos of my food make my mouth water every time I see them.

Roberto de Vicq de Cumptich, Leah Carlson-Stanisic, Mary Speaker, and the entire design team whose sense of style shines through from cover to cover.

Ann Cahn and Karen Lumley and the entire production staff at Morrow. Even last-minute changes never seem to faze these guys.

Carrie Weinberg, Corinne Alhadeff, Andrea Cerini, and everyone at Morrow who takes care of sales, marketing, and publicity. Without them this book might never have made it out the door.

Bethany Chamberlain, Glenn Muhr, Richard Pacifico, Claudia Vosper, and everyone at Spier-NY who never tired of trying yet another batch of peanut brittle, marshmallows, and nougat.

Dan Sanders, my painless dentist who got me through half a ton of sugar and vats of corn syrup with my smile intact.

Mark Scarbrough, my loving partner, best friend, discriminating taster, generous critic, and unwavering pillar of support. None of it would be possible without him.

INTRODUCTION

By THE AGE OF SIX, I was hooked. I loved to watch my pennies disappear into the red metal base of a gum ball machine. Where did they go? How did the gum balls make their way down the chute? By junior high school, I no longer cared. I saved my pennies for Doc's, a candy store where I could choose exactly what I wanted, from taffy to lollipops.

Traveling has introduced me to some of my new favorite sweet snacks. On my first day in Paris, I discovered *pâte de fruits*—chewy, intensely flavored fruit candies. I ate an entire kilo before I got back to my hotel. Every day I stopped in a *pâtisserie* near the cathedral of Notre Dame and bought all of their *orangettes*— strips of candied orange rind covered in bittersweet chocolate.

In New York, I've found traditional marzipan at the Elk Candy Company near the Metropolitan Museum of Art, wandered through the myriad chocolate shops from Europe that line Madison Avenue, and continue to marvel at the century-old stores specializing in dried fruits and nuts that dot the Lower East Side of the city.

I decided to tackle candy making in my own kitchen to add to the jams and cookies I always put in holiday packages. I started with lollipops. I found a set of metal molds at a local kitchenware store, complete with sticks, bags, and flavorings. But I didn't stop there. I tried making marshmallows and peanut brittle the following year. I finally tried my hand at *pâte de fruits* and (to my dentist's horror) homemade chewing gum.

Friends and family started asking for the recipes and I was more than happy to oblige. I am thrilled to be able to share all of my recipes with you and hope you enjoy making them as much as I have over the years. This collection of recipes follows the format of my previous *Ultimate Books, The Ultimate Ice Cream Book* and *The Ultimate Party Drink Book,* in which I offer you basic recipes followed by a series of easy-to-create variations.

Now your kitchen can always be filled with *everything* from peanut butter cups to pistachio bark, from coconut snowballs to butterscotch drops, and endless variations of your all-time favorites and your soon-to-be new favorite candies.

EQUIPMENT

CANDY THERMOMETERS

Most candy is made from sugar that has been cooked. At different temperatures, sugar takes on different properties, so measuring the temperature is the most important step in successful candy making.

There's no way around it: you must have a candy thermometer. Meat thermometers and instant-read thermometers just won't work because they are not designed to stand up to the continued high temperatures of candy making. They are also not designed to be clipped to the inside of a pan, which is where candy thermometers must be placed.

Readability is the most important feature to look for when buying a candy thermometer. If you have a hard time telling what temperature the thermometer shows in the store, don't buy it. A pot of boiling sugar syrup will only make it more difficult to read.

The best candy thermometers register 100 to 400°F in 2-degree increments. They clearly mark all the stages sugar reaches as it cooks: *thread, soft ball, firm ball, hard ball, soft crack*, and *hard crack*. I'll discuss these stages at more length under Techniques, page 10.

Two brands of thermometers that I have trusted for years are Taylor and Wilton. If you can't find them in your local cook-ware store, consult the Source Guide on page 242.

Before you use your new thermometer, test its accuracy by clipping it to the inside of a pan filled with water. Bring the water to a boil over high heat and make sure the thermometer registers 212°F. If it doesn't, bring it back to the store and get another one.

CHOCOLATE THERMOMETERS

Chocolate melts at low temperatures and requires a thermometer that reads 90°F or lower. I prefer to use a chocolate-melting thermometer rather than a candy thermometer because chocolate thermometers register from 40°F to 130°F. They're usually marked in 1-degree increments, making them more accurate. And after all, temperature accuracy is the key to successful candy making.

My chocolate thermometer is made by Component Design Northwest (model TCH 130). Check your local baking supply store or consult the Source Guide on page 242.

Some people melt chocolate without a special thermometer. Not a good idea, as the lack of accurate temperature measurement can lead to less than perfect results: burned chocolate or chocolate that has a cloudy or dull finish.

Both a candy thermometer and a separate chocolate thermometer are a wise investment for every candy maker.

CANDY MOLDS

Candy molds are the best-kept secret for beautiful, easy-to-make candy. Molds help you make lollipops, caramels, mints, and hard candies that are perfect every time. Some molds are made for shaping hot syrups, while other molds are made for shaping cool to warm candies like marzipan or tempered chocolate. Don't be misled by materials: not all hard-candy molds are made of metal. Some plastics can withstand very hot temperatures. When you purchase molds, remember to ask whether the mold is made for hard candy. If you try to pour a hot syrup into a mold made for chocolate or other low-temperature candies, you'll melt the mold and have a dangerous mess on your hands.

Pouring liquid candy into molds is easier to do from a pan with a pouring spout. If you don't have one, transfer your hot mixture to a Pyrex measuring cup with a spout and a handle.

You can also use a candy funnel to fill molds. Candy funnels have a handle plus a built-in stopper on the bottom that you control with your thumb. This makes filling molds quick and easy. Funnels can be found at cookware stores, or consult the Source Guide on page 242.

CHOCOLATE DIPPING TOOLS

Many recipes in this book call for dipping candy into tempered chocolate. I wrote these recipes for the home cook who may not have professional dipping tools. These are long-handled plastic or metal tools designed to dip particular candies into melted chocolate. Some have double prongs which are great for dipping truffles or other firm candies. Others have triple prongs, making them more suitable for marshmallows or other soft candy centers. Some have no prongs at all, but are shaped to hold specific fruits or nuts. I have seen candy dipping tools that have spirals on the end (which will give the candy a swirl pattern when it's flipped over), and others that have flat spatulalike ends for dipping cookies or crackers.

All my recipes describe how to dip candy into chocolate using tools you already have in your home, such as forks, tweezers, and toothpicks. If you want to try your hand at dipping candy with professional tools, consult the Source Guide on page 242 and follow the manufacturer's directions.

DOUBLE BOILER

A double boiler is a great tool for melting chocolate and other candy ingredients. It's a two-part pot. The bottom is filled with water, which is heated to produce steam. The top part fits snugly over the bottom and is heated by the steam in the bottom. Melting chocolate this way rather than over direct heat allows you to control the temperature better and avoids burning the chocolate. Double boilers are also great for melting fondant, caramels, butterscotch chips, and marshmallows.

If you don't have a double boiler, you can improvise. Any saucepan will do for the bottom, but I think a 3½-quart saucepan is the perfect size. Now choose a heatproof bowl or second saucepan that fits snugly over the bottom pan. *Snug* is the key word, because you don't want any steam to leak out and condense onto whatever you're melting.

KITCHEN SCALES

Kitchen scales are the best way to make sure you use the exact amount of chocolate required in each recipe. Kitchen scales are available at most cookware stores and come in two basic varieties. The first is spring-loaded. Look for spring-loaded scales that have a device that allows you to adjust the display to make sure that you always start at zero. I don't recommend buying a spring-loaded scale without this adjustable feature.

The other type of scale is electronic. It is very accurate and consistent. One of the benefits of electronic scales is that you can measure fractions of an ounce and switch between ounces and grams at the touch of a button. While professional electronic kitchen scales need to be plugged in, smaller versions designed for home use run on batteries.

Kitchen scales also make it easy to divide up a batch of candy for gift giving. Whether you make four kinds of fudge or seven kinds of brittle, you can be sure that everyone gets the same amount if you measure it out with a scale.

PASTRY BRUSHES

These resemble little paintbrushes and can be found in almost every cookware store. They come in sizes from ½ inch to 2 inches or larger. They are used for everything from greasing pans and molds to brushing melted chocolate into paper cups. I like to use brushes made from natural materials such as boar's hair or hog bristles. Nylon brushes are also available. Wash your pastry brush well after each use and let it dry completely before putting it away. Never put your pastry brush in the dishwasher or the bristles will dry out and can break off the next time you use the brush.

POTS AND PANS

When it comes to pans, copper has always been most chefs' choice for candy making because it conducts heat fast and evenly. But copper pans are not necessary for successful candy making. I have used heavy anodized aluminum pots and enameled cast-iron pans for years. I do have one copper pan with a pouring spout which makes filling candy molds easy. This is a luxury item in candy making and if you are looking for one, check your local cookware store or consult the Source Guide on page 242.

SCISSORS

A good pair of strong scissors is as important to candy making as knives are to cooking. Scissors are great for snipping taffy and caramel into bite-sized pieces, as well as for cutting parchment or wax paper to fit cookie sheets and pans. I keep a clean pair of scissors in the kitchen and don't use them for anything but cooking. Just remember to wash and dry them as you would any kitchen tool. I even put mine in the dishwasher.

WAX PAPER AND PARCHMENT

Some recipes in the book call for wax paper while others call for parchment. The papers are not interchangeable. Wax paper is great for all sorts of chocolate candies, but it will melt under the heat of peanut brittle and other hot sugar syrups. If you can't find parchment paper in your supermarket, consult the Source Guide on page 242.

WORK SURFACES

If you have marble or granite counters at home, you have a ready-made candy-making kitchen. If not, you can always buy marble slabs or tiles at your local flooring supply store. Remainder marble or granite tiles in 12-inch or 18-inch squares are often available at a fraction of their original cost.

A nonstick cookie sheet will also work if it is prepared according to the recipe.

My favorite nonstick surface is a thin, flexible, rubbery sheet called Silpat. It was designed for baking, but it works for candy making as well. Everything from chocolate bark to lollipops simply peels right off. Silpat is available at many cookware stores and from many of the sources listed in the Source Guide on page 242.

INGREDIENTS

YOUR CANDY WILL be only as good as the ingredients you use to make it. Buy the best you can comfortably afford in every category.

BUTTER

When butter is called for, it is always unsalted butter, sometimes called sweet butter on the label. The amount of salt added to salted butter varies from brand to brand. So unsalted butter gives you control of the amount of salt in the candy.

CHOCOLATE

For simplicity's sake, there are four types of chocolate called for in my recipes: white, milk, semisweet, and unsweetened (or baking) chocolate.

High-quality white chocolate contains cocoa butter, sugar, and vanilla flavoring. Other ingredients can be added, such as milk solids and lecithin. White baking chips are usually not made from white chocolate, but they taste similar and can be used in any of my recipes that call for white chocolate. White chocolate has a short shelf life (about 9 months), so check the package for any expiration date.

High-quality milk chocolate contains cocoa butter, sugar, cocoa solids and liquor, as well as milk, milk solids, or milk fat. (Chocolate liquor contains no alcohol, but is the substance that remains from the cocoa bean when most of the cocoa butter is removed.) Milk chocolate has a longer shelf life than white chocolate (about 1 year). Milk chocolate chips can be used in any of my recipes calling for milk chocolate.

Semisweet chocolate is a kind of dark chocolate and contains no dairy. There is a wide variety of dark chocolates to choose from. They include semisweet, bittersweet, and extra-bitter. They all have varying ratios of sugar, cocoa butter, and cocoa solids or liquor. They are also similar in taste and are interchangeable in all of my recipes that call for semisweet chocolate. Semisweet chips can also be used. Dark chocolates have the longest shelf life (about 2 years).

Unsweetened (or baking) chocolate contains no sugar and is not interchangeable with any other chocolate.

COCOA POWDER

Cocoa can be found in two forms, regular and Dutch processed. Dutch processing adds alkali to the cocoa to help it dissolve in recipes. Either kind can be used in any of my recipes calling for cocoa powder.

COCONUT

Coconut is readily available in most markets as sweetened shredded coconut or sweetened chopped coconut. Many recipes call for unsweetened coconut chips or shreds. You can often find unsweetened coconut at Latin markets and Asian markets, or consult the Source Guide on page 242. If you want to make your own shredded, unsweetened coconut, follow the recipe on page 211.

CORNSTARCH

Cornstarch is used as a thickener for candies such as Turkish Delight. It gives candy a sticky and somewhat gummy consistency. It is also used for coating some candies such as nougat because it imparts no additional sweetness yet allows for easy handling.

CORN SYRUP

This is the most widely used sweetener in the United States. It is in almost every processed sweet we eat. It helps keep sugar from crystallizing and makes candy smoother and taste "creamier." As its name implies, it is derived from corn and is available in dark and light forms. Look for it in the baking aisle of your supermarket.

CREAM OF TARTAR

Cream of tartar, when added to some recipes, makes the candy creamier by inhibiting the sugar from crystallizing. It is sometimes added to egg whites to keep them from drying out when they are beaten. Look for it in the spice rack at your local supermarket.

DRIED FRUIT

Just as you would with fresh fruit, smell dried fruit before you buy it. It should smell sweet and fragrant. Dried fruit should also be plump and moist, not hard and leathery. You will not be able to smell commercially packaged dried fruit such as raisins or prunes, so stick to brand names for the best quality.

EVAPORATED MILK

This canned milk product is milk with much of the water removed. It's a pantry staple and contains no sugar. It's available in full-fat, low-fat, and nonfat varieties. My recipes specify which kind to use.

FLAVORINGS AND EXTRACTS

Candy flavorings can be found in almost any supermarket. In the spice aisle, you'll find extracts and flavorings like almond, coconut, banana, lemon, orange, mint, and anise.

Fruit flavors are often available in natural and artificial form, while more unusual flavors, such as bubble gum, tutti-frutti, cheesecake, or peanut butter, are available only in artificial form. Consult the Source Guide on page 242 for an extensive collection of natural and artificial flavor suppliers.

Candy flavorings are usually either oil-based or alcohol-based. Alcohol-based flavorings can be used in any kind of candy. Oil-based flavorings do not incorporate completely into hot cooked sugar syrups and are better for chocolate and other low-temperature candies such as fondants and fudge.

FOOD COLORING

The most common form of food coloring is the little box of four liquid colors (red, blue, yellow, and green) that is available in almost every supermarket. Consult the side of the box for information on blending colors to create the color you need. Professional food coloring comes in gel or paste form and is available in hundreds of ready-mixed colors. White coloring, also called liquid whitener, makes candy opaque and creamy looking. For professional food coloring suppliers, consult the Source Guide on page 242.

GELATIN

Granulated, unflavored gelatin is the most common variety of gelatin available. Professional chefs use gelatin leaves, but they are hard to find and not used here.

GOLDEN SYRUP

This amber liquid is the byproduct of sugar refining. It has an unmistakable flavor that I find slightly sweeter than white sugar or corn syrup. The most common brand is Lyle's Golden Syrup, available in jars or cans in most supermarkets or gourmet stores.

HONEY

There are as many kinds of honey as there are flowers and trees. Remember that the darker the honey, the stronger its flavor. The most common honey is a mild-tasting clover honey. I prefer stronger and unique flavors like orange blossom or lavender.

MAPLE SYRUP

Pancake syrup is not maple syrup. Real maple syrup is boiled sap from the maple tree. It comes in light, medium, and dark amber. I prefer medium or dark for cooking. The flavor of light amber maple syrup is not strong enough to cut through most recipes.

NUTS AND SEEDS

Nuts and seeds are usually available roasted or raw, shelled or unshelled, salted or unsalted. Every recipe specifies what kind of nuts or seeds to use. If you cannot find roasted nuts and you need them, roast (or toast) them yourself following the directions on page 12. Shelling nuts is tedious work but necessary if you cannot find the kind of nuts you need already shelled. A metal nutcracker or small hammer is the best tool for cracking hard nuts such as walnuts and almonds. Your hands are just fine for softer nuts and seeds such as pistachios, peanuts, pumpkin seeds, or sunflower seeds.

SUGARS

White granulated sugar is the most common and called-for sugar in this book. It is the kind we all buy in five-pound bags at the supermarket.

Brown sugar comes in two varieties: light and dark. Each one gets its color from molasses. Dark brown sugar contains nearly twice the molasses of light brown sugar. Brown sugar can clump and harden if not stored airtight. If this happens, wrap the sugar in plastic and microwave it on high for 10 seconds or until it softens. If you don't have a microwave, you can wrap the sugar in aluminum foil and place it in a 350° F oven for 5 minutes or until softened.

Confectioners' sugar is a mixture of 97 percent powdered sugar (a pulverized form of sugar) and 3 percent cornstarch. The most common variety comes in 1-pound boxes and is labeled "Confectioners' 10X Powdered."

Superfine sugar is sometimes referred to as instant-dissolving sugar or bar sugar. It is perfect for coating jelly candies as it doesn't add too much crunch. It is also often used in meringue because it dissolves so well in beaten egg whites.

SWEETENED CONDENSED MILK

This is another pantry staple that is made from milk cooked with sugar until it is thick and rich. Sweetened condensed milk is available in full-fat, low-fat, and nonfat varieties. It is also available in chocolate flavor.

VANILLA EXTRACT

Unless otherwise called for, never use imitation vanilla flavoring. Pure vanilla extract will make your candy taste better. Vanilla extract from Madagascar is my personal favorite. I find Mexican vanilla extracts to be weaker in flavor. A few American manufacturers make double-strength vanilla, which is a real treat if you can find it. Look for Adams brand, a double-strength vanilla that is available in many supermarkets. Only in my white truffle recipe do I call for imitation vanilla flavoring, but in a clear form called clear vanilla. I use it to help keep these truffles white. For vanilla of all kinds, check the Source Guide on page 242.

TECHNIQUES

CANDY TEMPERATURES AT HIGH ALTITUDES

If you live at a high altitude, make sure that you know what temperature water boils at, and test your new thermometer for that number. Note the difference between the boiling point of water at your altitude and 212°F. Subtract this difference from the various temperatures called for throughout this book.

COLD-WATER TESTING

Before thermometers became household tools, candy makers tested the temperature of cooked sugar syrup by dropping a small amount of it into cold water. They found that a thread will form when the water-cooled sugar syrup reaches 230°F. A soft ball will form if you pinch the water-cooled sugar between your fingers after it reaches 240°F. A firm ball will form when the water-cooled syrup is rolled between your fingers after reaching 248 to 250°F, and a hard ball will form after 260°F. At 275°F, the water-cooled sugar forms a mass that softly cracks when bent. At 300°F, the water-cooled sugar reaches hard crack, forming a hard piece of candy that resembles lollipops, sucking candy, and toffee. Over

310°F, the sugar turns amber. When you're cooking sugar for a recipe that requires this level of heat, there is no need for a thermometer or a cold-water test. Your eyes can tell you when the sugar is done.

Many chefs and home cooks still use this cold-water test, but I highly recommend a thermometer.

MEASURING CHOCOLATE

Candy making is just like chemistry. If you change the ratio of ingredients, your candy will not come out right. It is very important to use the exact amount of each ingredient required, especially chocolate. For best accuracy, the amount of chocolate required is always given in my recipes by weight in ounces. Don't be fooled: chocolate chips (white, milk, or semisweet) are sold in bags that tell you how much they weigh, but it's often hard to get an exact weight when you are dividing a bag. Bars of chocolate also tell you how much they weigh, but are difficult to divide with accuracy. And if you are buying chocolate in bulk from a candy supply store, it is easy to divide up the chocolate, but there is no way to measure the amount you need other than with a kitchen scale (see page 4).

CHOPPING CHOCOLATE

Before melting chocolate, it is important to chop it into small pieces, about the size of whole almonds. This will help the chocolate melt evenly and quickly.

Chocolate can be chopped by hand using a large kitchen knife on a cutting board, or it can be chopped in a food processor. If you do use a food processor, pulse the machine on and off until the chocolate is chopped to the desired size. If you let it go too long, the chocolate will be pulverized.

Chocolate chips (large, regular, or mini) do not need to be chopped.

MELTING AND TEMPERING CHOCOLATE

When you melt chocolate for candy making, you must use a double boiler (see page 3) to help you control the heat and temper the chocolate. That means the chocolate is slowly melted and then cooled with constant stirring until it falls back to 88 to 90°F for semi-sweet chocolate, and 86 to 88°F for milk or white chocolate. Properly tempered chocolate will have a smooth, glossy appearance and will harden quickly and evenly.

When you use a double boiler to melt chocolate, you should bring the water in the bottom pan to a boil and then remove the pan from the heat. The water will still be hot enough to melt the chocolate. If the water is still boiling or simmering, too much steam will be created and the chocolate will melt too quickly and can become too hot, changing its taste.

Be sure that the seal between the top and bottom pans is tight. Any steam that leaks out can cause water to condense onto the melting chocolate. Even a few drops can cause the chocolate to seize (that is, to congeal into a hard clump on the bottom of the pan), making the chocolate unusable for candy making. Beating in additional liquid (such as melted butter, or even more hot water), 1 tablespoon at a time, can help smooth out the chocolate, but the chocolate won't set up correctly when cooled. If your chocolate seizes and you fix it in this manner, you can still serve it as chocolate sauce over ice cream or cake.

Properly tempered chocolate stays shiny as it cools, if it's left at room temperature, about 65 to 75°F. But chocolate can be temperamental, and even tempered chocolate can end up with a dull or gray appearance if it cools too slowly or too quickly. Since this doesn't affect the taste, a quick sprinkling of cocoa powder or confectioners' sugar will fix any surface imperfections.

When you cool candy made with tempered chocolate, you can speed up the cooling process by placing the candy in the refrigerator for 10 minutes, but no longer. Continue to cool the candy at room temperature. This technique is great on hot days if you don't have air-conditioning.

Chocolate will hold up better on hot days or in warmer climates with the addition of specific fats, such as partially hydrogenated palm seed oil. Commercial chocolate suppliers make *coating choco-*

late or *summer coating*, which contains these additional fats. This type of chocolate doesn't always taste great on its own, but it does come in handy in hot weather.

On very hot days, I sometimes mix high-quality chocolate with a little of this coating chocolate or summer coating to create the perfect combination of taste and texture. I get the best of both worlds with a ratio of 1 part coating chocolate to 4 parts high-quality chocolate. Coating chocolate and summer coating are available from candy supply stores, or consult the Source Guide on page 242.

TOASTING NUTS AND COCONUT

Preheat your oven to 350°F. Spread the nuts or coconut on a cookie sheet and bake for 10 minutes or until they turn a light brown. Stir the nuts or coconut every few minutes to help them brown evenly. Larger nuts will take longer to brown than smaller nuts. And the sugar in sweetened shredded coconut will make the coconut brown fast. So it's important to keep an eye on whatever it is you're toasting to help prevent it from burning.

WEATHER

Chocolate is hard to work with in the middle of summer without air-conditioning, and hard candies and lollipops can get sticky when it's humid. Some candies just won't turn out well if the barometer says it's a low-pressure day. If the weather is giving you a bad hair day, just imagine what it's going to do to your divinity, nougat, or taffy! But there are always hundreds of other treats to make.

AVOIDING AND TREATING BURNS

The temperatures you are dealing with in candy making are extraordinarily high. Spill or splash even the smallest amount of boiling sugar syrup on your skin and you'll have a nasty burn. Always work with a bowl of ice water nearby. If you do accidentally burn your hand, plunge it immediately into the ice water. If you've burned something other than your hand, immediately place ice on the burned area. If the burn is severe, apply ice and call 911 for emergency help. Keeping an aloe vera plant on hand is also a good idea. Break off a leaf and squeeze the jelly onto the burned area after cooling the burn down with ice. The ice will help prevent blisters and further damage, while the aloe vera gel will promote healing. If you have even a mild burn and the pain persists more than a few hours, seek medical attention immediately.

Candy is for kids, but candy making is for adults. Your kids should only help you decorate cooled candy, and they can always enjoy the fruits of your labor.

CANDIES FOR SPECIAL OCCASIONS

BIRTHDAYS

Birthday Party Chocolate Potato Chips
Caramel Corn
Chocolate Cups
Chocolate Pretzels
Chocolate Taffy
Fudge In a Minute
Gummy Bears
Lollipops
Marshmallow Crispy Squares
Popcorn Balls
Saltwater Taffy

CHRISTMAS

Bourbon Balls
Chocolate-Dipped Candy Canes
Chestnut Candy
Chocolate Christmas Lollipops
Christmas Candy
Christmas Candy Ornaments
Christmas Coconut Snowballs
Christmas Cream Cheese Mints
Christmas Divinity
Christmas Lollipops
Date Roll
Holiday Mint Chocolate Bark
Marzipan Pinecones
Peanut Brittle
Sugarplums

EASTER

Apricot Jewels
Chocolate Easter Lollipops
Chocolate Palm Leaves
Easter Candy
Easter Cream Cheese Mints
Orange *Pâte de Fruits*

HALLOWEEN

Candy Apples
Caramel Apples
Chocolate Spiderwebs
Halloween Butterscotch Bark
Halloween Candy
Halloween Cream Cheese Mints
Halloween Divinity
Halloween Marshmallow Pops
Halloween Marshmallows
Pumpkinseed Crunch

HANUKKAH

Chickpea Candy
Chocolate Hanukkah Lollipops
Coconut Snowballs
Halvah
Hanukkah Cream Cheese Mints
Orangettes
Sesame Crunch

PASSOVER

Chocolate Matzo
Chocolate Meringue Kisses
Coconut Brittle
Jewish S'mores
Marzipan Potatoes
Meringue Kisses
Trail Mix

THANKSGIVING

Apple Candy
Chocolate Autumn Leaves
Cranberry Almond Bark
Maple Fudge
Pecan Roll
Pumpkin Pecan Candy
Rum Raisin Pralines
Spiced Fruit Bars
Squash Candy

VALENTINE'S DAY

Chocolate Cherries
Chocolate Creams
Chocolate Valentine's Lollipops
Truffles
Valentine's Cream Cheese Mints
Valentine's Marshmallows

QUICK *and* EASY
S w e e t s

THIS CHAPTER CONTAINS RECIPES FOR chocolates and other candies that even beginners can make. In fact, you'll find that if you can boil water, you can make these candies. They require very few ingredients and little time. They're just perfect for last-minute treats when unexpected company drops by or when time is at a premium. Just imagine chocolate cups filled with jelly beans at your next kids' birthday party. Or what about rolled marshmallow pops at the next office party? And granola peanut butter trail bars will make your next long car trip a pleasure. It's all here, just waiting to be enjoyed.

ALMOND BARK

Barks have always been popular candies to make because they're easy and versatile. Traditionally, you break them into irregular shapes resembling peeled tree bark. You can make them from almost any combination of chocolates, dried fruits, and nuts. In this version, milk chocolate is mixed with almonds (whole, slivered, or sliced).

12 ounces milk chocolate, roughly chopped, or 12 ounces milk chocolate chips

¼ pound almonds (whole, slivered, or sliced), toasted (see page 12)

Butter or margarine for greasing the cookie sheet

1· Butter a large cookie sheet and line it with wax paper. Set it aside.

2· Melt 6 ounces of the milk chocolate in the top of a double boiler set over hot water. If you don't have a double boiler, simply place the chocolate in a bowl that fits snugly over a pot of hot water.

3· When the chocolate has melted completely, remove the top part of the double boiler or the bowl from the hot water. Add the remaining 6 ounces of milk chocolate and stir until all of the chocolate is melted and smooth.

4· Insert a candy thermometer or chocolate thermometer into the melted chocolate. Its temperature should be 86 to 88°F. If the chocolate is too cold, place it back over the hot water until the temperature reaches 86 to 88°F. If it is too hot, let it cool until the desired temperature is reached.

5· Add the almonds all at once and mix with a wooden spoon until they are thoroughly coated with chocolate.

6· Pour the chocolate mixture onto the prepared cookie sheet and spread it with a spatula or wooden spoon to about a ½-inch thickness. Don't worry if the chocolate doesn't reach the sides and corners of the cookie sheet; a free-form shape is preferred.

7. Let the bark set up and harden at room temperature, about 4 hours. The cooler your room's temperature, the faster the bark will harden. You can speed up the process by first placing the bark in the refrigerator for 10 minutes, but no longer.

8. Grab the edges of the cooled bark and peel it off the wax paper in one piece, if possible. Break it with your hands into irregular pieces, about the size of a credit card. Store the candy in an airtight container at room temperature for up to 1 month.

VARIATIONS

DARK ALMOND BARK Substitute 12 ounces semisweet chocolate for the milk chocolate.

WHITE ALMOND BARK Substitute 12 ounces white chocolate for the milk chocolate.

The following variations work with the base recipe or with either of the preceding chocolate variations.

APRICOT ALMOND BARK Add ½ cup chopped dried apricots with the almonds to the melted chocolate.

CHERRY ALMOND BARK Add ¼ cup whole dried cherries with the almonds to the melted chocolate.

CINNAMON ALMOND BARK Add 1 teaspoon ground cinnamon with the almonds to the melted chocolate.

CRANBERRY ALMOND BARK Add ¼ cup whole dried cranberries with the almonds to the melted chocolate.

DATE ALMOND BARK Add ¼ cup coarsely chopped dried dates with the almonds to the melted chocolate.

RED HOT ALMOND BARK Add ¼ cup red hot cinnamon candies with the almonds to the melted chocolate.

ROSE ALMOND BARK Add ¼ cup crumbled candied rose petals with the almonds to the melted chocolate.

BOURBON BALLS

These traditional candies are only as good as the bourbon you use to make them—so buy the best bourbon you can comfortably afford. I include them in every holiday dessert table. They're great for buffets because you can pick them up with your fingers and eat them in one bite (or two), no plates required.

> 25 vanilla wafers, such as Nilla Wafers
>
> ¼ cup bourbon, such as Jack Daniels Black Label or Maker's Mark
>
> 1 cup confections' sugar, sifted
>
> 1 cup finely chopped pecans
>
> 3 tablespoons cocoa powder plus additional for coating
>
> 1½ tablespoons light corn syrup

1· Roughly crumble the vanilla wafers into a large mixing bowl. Add the bourbon and allow the mixture to soften, stirring once or twice, about 2 minutes.

2· Add the confections' sugar, pecans, 3 tablespoons cocoa powder, and corn syrup. Mix with your hands or a wooden spoon until all the ingredients are thoroughly combined.

3· Place the batter in the refrigerator for 10 to 15 minutes to make it easier to shape.

4· Roll 1 tablespoon of batter between your palms to create a ball. Repeat with the remaining batter. Roll the bourbon balls in cocoa. Store the candy in layers, separated by wax paper, in an airtight container in the refrigerator for up to 1 week.

VARIATIONS

BRANDY BALLS Substitute ¼ cup brandy for the bourbon.

CHERRY BOURBON BALLS Press 1 candied cherry (green or red) inside each bourbon ball before rolling it in cocoa.

CHOCOLATE BOURBON BALLS Substitute 25 chocolate wafers for the vanilla wafers.

RUM BALLS Substitute ¼ cup gold rum for the bourbon.

RUM GINGER BALLS Substitute 25 gingersnaps for the vanilla wafers and substitute ¼ cup gold rum for the bourbon.

RUM PINEAPPLE BALLS Substitute ¼ cup gold rum for the bourbon. Press one ½-inch piece dried pineapple inside each rum ball before rolling it in cocoa.

WALNUT BALLS Substitute 1 cup chopped walnuts for the pecans.

WHITE BOURBON BALLS Substitute confections' sugar for the cocoa powder to coat the balls.

BUTTERSCOTCH BARK

Butterscotch chips are rich and intense. A little goes a long way, so break this bark into very small pieces. To crumble hard butterscotch candy, place it in a doubled paper or plastic bag and hit it a few times with a heavy pot. But if you overdo it, you'll have candy powder instead of candy crumbs. Don't use your food processor—it will not crush the hard candy evenly, leaving you with powder and chunks.

12 ounces butterscotch chips

¾ cup crumbled hard butterscotch candy (see above)

Butter or margarine for greasing the cookie sheet

1· Butter a large cookie sheet and line it with wax paper.

2· Melt 6 ounces of the butterscotch chips in the top of a double boiler set over hot water. If you don't have a double boiler, simply place the chips in a bowl that fits snugly over a pot of hot water.

3· When the chips have melted completely, remove the top part of the double boiler or the bowl from the hot water. Add the remaining 6 ounces of chips and stir until all the chips are melted and the mixture is smooth.

4· Add the crumbled candy and stir with a wooden spoon until the candy is completely covered in melted butterscotch.

5· Pour the butterscotch mixture onto the prepared cookie sheet and spread it with a spatula or wooden spoon to about a ½-inch thickness. Don't worry if the mixture doesn't reach the sides and corners of the cookie sheet; a free-form shape is preferred.

6· Let the bark set up and harden at room temperature, about 4 hours, or set it in the refrigerator for about 1 hour.

7· Grab the edges of the cooled bark and peel it off the wax paper in one piece, if possible. Break it with your hands into irregular pieces, about 2 inches each. Store the candy in an airtight container at room temperature for up to 1 month.

APRICOT BUTTERSCOTCH BARK Substitute 1 cup chopped dried apricots for the crumbled hard butterscotch candy.

BANANA BUTTERSCOTCH BARK Substitute ¾ cup chopped dried banana for the crumbled butterscotch candy.

CHOCOLATE COOKIE BUTTERSCOTCH BARK Substitute ¾ cup roughly chopped Oreo cookies for the crumbled butterscotch candy.

GINGER BUTTERSCOTCH BARK Reduce the amount of butterscotch candy to ½ cup. Add ⅓ cup finely chopped candied ginger with the crumbled butterscotch candy.

GINGER RAISIN BUTTERSCOTCH BARK Substitute 1 cup golden raisins and ¼ cup finely chopped candied ginger for the crumbled butterscotch candy.

GOLDEN RAISIN BUTTERSCOTCH BARK Substitute 1¼ cups golden raisins for the crumbled butterscotch candy.

HALLOWEEN BUTTERSCOTCH BARK Substitute ¾ cup whole candy corn for the crumbled butterscotch candy.

MARSHMALLOW BUTTERSCOTCH BARK Add ¾ cup miniature marshmallows with the crumbled butterscotch candy.

PEANUT BUTTERSCOTCH BARK Substitute ¾ cup salted peanuts for the crumbled butterscotch candy.

PEANUT RAISIN BUTTERSCOTCH BARK Substitute ½ cup salted peanuts and ½ cup dark raisins for the crumbled butterscotch candy.

CHOCOLATE CUPS

If you've ever seen desserts served in chocolate cups and wondered how it's done, here's the secret. You can make them in any size and fill them with ice cream, sorbet, chocolate mousse, or even small candies. They're great for birthday parties, for kids of all ages.

> 12 ounces semisweet chocolate, coarsely chopped, or 12 ounces semisweet chocolate chips
> 12 paper muffin cups, 2½ inches each

1· Melt 6 ounces of the semisweet chocolate in the top of a double boiler set over hot water. If you don't have a double boiler, simply place the chocolate in a bowl that fits snugly over a pot of hot water.

2· When the chocolate has melted completely, remove the top part of the double boiler or the bowl from the hot water. Add the remaining 6 ounces of semisweet chocolate and stir until all of the chocolate is melted and smooth.

3· Insert a candy thermometer or chocolate thermometer into the melted chocolate. Its temperature should be 88 to 90°F. If the chocolate is too cold, place it back over the hot water until the temperature reaches 88 to 90°F. If it is too hot, let it cool until the desired temperature is reached.

4· Double the paper cups to make them sturdier. Using a 1-inch pastry brush, paint the insides of the muffin cups with the melted chocolate to about a ⅛-inch thickness. Setting the cups into a muffin tin will help them hold their shape while they cool. Place the cups in the refrigerator for 30 minutes to set up.

5· Remove the cups from the tin and carefully peel away the paper. The chocolate cups will be very fragile. Store them in a single layer in an airtight container at room temperature for up to 2 weeks.

BLACK-AND-WHITE CHOCOLATE CUPS Paint the insides of the paper cups with one coat of semisweet chocolate and allow them to set up as directed. Then paint the insides of the chocolate cups with melted white chocolate and repeat the process.

CHOCOLATE BOWLS Instead of using paper cups, blow up 6 to 8 small washed and dried balloons to about 6 inches in diameter. Dip the balloons into the melted chocolate, about 3 inches up the sides. Set the balloons on wax paper and place them in the refrigerator to allow the chocolate to harden quickly, about 20 minutes. Dip the balloons a second time after the first coating has set. Place the balloons back on the wax paper and return them to the refrigerator to allow the second coating to harden. To remove the balloons, pop each with a pin at the top, where the balloon is not covered in chocolate. Peel the deflated balloon away from the chocolate.

CIRCUS CHOCOLATE CUPS Substitute 12 ounces white chocolate for the dark chocolate. Add 2 to 3 drops food coloring of your choice before painting the cups.

MILK CHOCOLATE CUPS Substitute 12 ounces milk chocolate for the dark chocolate.

MINI CHOCOLATE CUPS Use small paper candy cups, about 1 inch, instead of paper muffin cups.

MINT CHOCOLATE CUPS Add 2 teaspoons peppermint extract or 4 drops peppermint oil to the melted chocolate before painting the paper cups. If desired, sprinkle the painted cups with ½ cup finely crushed peppermint candies before allowing the chocolate to harden.

NUTTY CHOCOLATE CUPS After painting the cups with one coat of chocolate, sprinkle the bottoms with finely chopped peanuts, almonds, or hazelnuts. When set, paint with a second layer of chocolate to cover the nuts.

WHITE CHOCOLATE CUPS Substitute 12 ounces white chocolate for the dark chocolate.

CHOCOLATE-DIPPED CANDY CANES

Sure, candy canes are pretty on their own. But dipping them in melted chocolate and decorating them with brightly colored sugar makes them holiday showstoppers. They make great holiday gifts, and as a bonus, they're also a lot of fun to make with kids.

> 1 cup red colored sugar
>
> 1 cup green colored sugar
>
> 12 ounces white chocolate, roughly chopped, or 12 ounces white chocolate chips
>
> 24 large striped candy canes
>
> Butter or margarine for greasing the cookie sheet

1· Butter a cookie sheet and line with wax paper. Place the sugars on two different plates and set aside.

2· Melt 6 ounces of the white chocolate in the top of a double boiler set over hot water. If you don't have a double boiler, simply place the chocolate in a bowl that fits snugly over a pot of hot water.

3· When the chocolate has melted completely, remove the top part of the double boiler or the bowl from the hot water. Add the remaining 6 ounces of white chocolate and stir until all of the chocolate is melted and smooth.

4· Insert a candy thermometer or chocolate thermometer into the melted chocolate. Its temperature should be 86 to 88°F. If the chocolate is too cold, place it back over the hot water until the temperature reaches 86 to 88°F. If it is too hot, let it cool until the desired temperature is reached.

5· Dip one candy cane at a time into the melted chocolate, about halfway up. Let the excess chocolate drip back into the bowl, then immediately roll the cane in either the red or the green sugar, until the chocolate is covered with the sugar. Set on the prepared cookie sheet and place in the refrigerator until the chocolate sets up, about 30 minutes.

6· Store the candy canes in an airtight container at room temperature.

VARIATIONS

MILK CHOCOLATE–DIPPED CANDY CANES Substitute 12 ounces milk chocolate for the white chocolate.

SEMISWEET CHOCOLATE–DIPPED CANDY CANES Substitute 12 ounces semisweet chocolate chips for the white chips.

The following variations work with the base recipe or with either of the preceding chocolate variations.

CONFETTI-DIPPED CANDY CANES Substitute candy confetti in any color or in mixed colors for the colored sugar.

DOUBLE MINT–DIPPED CANDY CANES Substitute 2 cups finely crushed peppermint candy (or candy canes) for the colored sugars.

GLITTERING DIPPED CANDY CANES Omit the colored sugars. Use a small paintbrush to paint edible gold or silver dust onto the set chocolate. (For edible gold or silver dust, see the Source Guide, page 242.)

NUTTY DIPPED CANDY CANES Substitute 2 cups finely chopped nuts for the colored sugars.

RAINBOW-DIPPED CANDY CANES Colored sugar comes in almost every conceivable color: pink, yellow, blue, purple, black, orange, or lavender. Use every color in the rainbow if you desire, or pick the colors that go best with your holiday decorations.

CHOCOLATE-DIPPED DRIED FRUIT

Dried fruit should always be plump and moist, not hard and leathery. The fruit should smell sweet and fragrant. In my opinion, a glass of sweet dessert wine and a chocolate-dipped piece of dried fruit is the perfect dessert.

16 ounces semisweet chocolate, roughly chopped, or 16 ounces semisweet chocolate chips

24 Australian glazed apricots, dried apple slices, dried black mission figs, dried pineapple slices, dried pitted dates, dried peaches, or dried pears

Butter or margarine for greasing the cookie sheet

1· Butter a large cookie sheet and line it with wax paper. Set aside.

2· Melt 8 ounces of the semisweet chocolate in the top of a double boiler set over hot water. If you don't have a double boiler, simply place the chocolate in a bowl that fits snugly over a pot of hot water.

3· When the chocolate has melted completely, remove the top part of the double boiler or the bowl from the hot water. Add the remaining 8 ounces of semisweet chocolate, and stir until all of the chocolate is melted and smooth.

4· Insert a candy thermometer or chocolate thermometer into the melted chocolate. Its temperature should be 88 to 90°F. If the chocolate is too cold, place it back over the hot water until the temperature reaches 88 to 90°F. If it is too hot, let it cool until the desired temperature is reached.

5· Hold the dried fruit by the stem, if it has one, and dip the fruit into the melted chocolate up to the stem. If the dried fruit has no stem, simply hold the fruit at the top and dip it into the melted chocolate three-quarters of the way up. Your fingers should not get covered in chocolate.

6· After dipping each piece, set it on the prepared cookie sheet. Repeat the process with the remaining dried fruit. If the chocolate gets too shallow to dip all the fruit, use a 1-inch pastry brush to paint the fruit with the melted chocolate, or use a spoon to drizzle the melted chocolate over the fruit.

7· Allow the dipped fruit to sit at room temperature until the chocolate hardens, about 4 hours. The cooler your room's temperature, the faster the chocolate will harden. You can speed up the process by placing the dipped fruit in the refrigerator for 10 minutes, but no longer.

8· When the chocolate is set, peel the fruits off the wax paper and store them in layers, separated by wax paper, in an airtight container at room temperature for up to 2 weeks.

VARIATIONS

MILK CHOCOLATE–DIPPED DRIED FRUIT Substitute 16 ounces milk chocolate for the semisweet chocolate.

WHITE CHOCOLATE–DIPPED DRIED FRUIT Substitute 16 ounces white chocolate for the semisweet chocolate.

The following variations work with the base recipe or with either of the preceding chocolate variations.

CHOCOLATE APPLES WITH WALNUTS Use only 24 dried apple slices, and sprinkle the dipped slices with finely chopped walnuts before the chocolate sets.

CHOCOLATE APRICOTS WITH HAZELNUTS Use only 24 Australian glazed apricots, and sprinkle the dipped apricots with finely chopped hazelnuts before the chocolate sets.

CHOCOLATE DATES WITH ALMONDS Use only 24 dried pitted dates. Stuff a large almond into each date before dipping into the melted chocolate.

CHOCOLATE HAZELNUT FIGS Use only 24 dried figs. Stuff one or two large hazelnuts inside each fig, from the bottom, before dipping it into the melted chocolate.

CHOCOLATE PEACHES WITH ALMONDS Use only 24 dried peaches, and sprinkle the dipped peaches with sliced almonds before the chocolate sets.

CHOCOLATE PEARS WITH PISTACHIOS Use only 24 dried pears, and sprinkle the dipped pears with finely chopped pistachio nuts before the chocolate sets.

CHOCOLATE-DIPPED MARSHMALLOW POPS

MAKES 24 POPS

If you love chocolate-covered marshmallows and you love lollipops, you will really love these simple treats. While the pops are delicious right from the refrigerator, they're even better from the freezer!

> 16 ounces white chocolate, coarsely chopped, or 16 ounces white chocolate chips
>
> 24 regular marshmallows
>
> 24 lollipop sticks
>
> 1 cup M&M's candies, plain
>
> Butter or margarine for greasing the cookie sheet

1· Butter a large cookie sheet and line it with wax paper. Set it aside.

2· Melt 8 ounces of the white chocolate in the top of a double boiler set over hot water. If you don't have a double boiler, simply place the chocolate in a bowl that fits snugly over a pot of hot water.

3· When the chocolate has melted completely, remove the top part of the double boiler or the bowl from the hot water. Add the remaining 8 ounces of white chocolate and stir until all of the chocolate is melted and smooth.

4· Insert a candy thermometer or chocolate thermometer into the melted chocolate. Its temperature should be 86 to 88°F. If the chocolate is too cold, place it back over the hot water until the temperature reaches 86 to 88°F. If it is too hot, let it cool until the desired temperature is reached.

5· Insert one lollipop stick into each marshmallow. Dip the marshmallows, one at a time, into the melted chocolate, being sure to cover the entire marshmallow. Use a tablespoon or 1-inch pastry brush to help, if necessary. Immediately sprinkle each marshmallow with the M&M's candies. The candy will stick to the melted chocolate. Place the pops on the prepared cookie sheet.

6. Place the pops in the refrigerator, for at least ½ hour, to allow the chocolate to harden, then store them in an airtight container in the refrigerator or in the freezer for up to 1 month.

VARIATIONS

CARAMEL MARSHMALLOW POPS Substitute 16 ounces caramel candies for the white chocolate.

MILK CHOCOLATE MARSHMALLOW POPS Substitute 16 ounces milk chocolate for the white chocolate.

SEMISWEET CHOCOLATE MARSHMALLOW POPS Substitute 16 ounces semisweet chocolate for the white chocolate.

The following variations work with the base recipe or with any of the preceding variations.

CANDY BAR MARSHMALLOW POPS Substitute 1 cup roughly crumbled candy bars, such as Butterfingers, Nestlé Crunch bars, Fifth Avenue, or Clark bars, for the M&M's.

CHOCOLATE CHIP MARSHMALLOW POPS Substitute 1 cup miniature chocolate chips for the M&M's.

NUTTY MARSHMALLOW POPS Substitute 1 cup roughly chopped nuts for the M&M's.

POTATO CHIP MARSHMALLOW POPS Substitute 1 cup lightly crushed potato chips for the M&M's.

RAISIN MARSHMALLOW POPS Substitute 1 cup whole raisins (dark or golden) for the M&M's.

CHOCOLATE-DIPPED STRAWBERRIES AND OTHER FRESH FRUITS

MAKES 24 PIECES

Chocolate-dipped strawberries have become a staple in every high-end candy store, and are served in every fancy restaurant coast-to-coast. Now you can make them along with other chocolate-dipped fruits at home. I prefer to store them in the refrigerator to help keep them fresh. I also like the contrast between the hard cold chocolate and the sweet soft fruit.

> 16 ounces semisweet chocolate, coarsely chopped, or 16 ounces semisweet chocolate chips
>
> 24 large strawberries with stems attached
>
> Butter or margarine for greasing the cookie sheet

1· Butter a large cookie sheet and line it with wax paper. Set aside.

2· Melt 8 ounces of the semisweet chocolate in the top of a double boiler set over hot water. If you don't have a double boiler, simply place the chocolate in a bowl that fits snugly over a pot of hot water.

3· When the chocolate has melted completely, remove the top part of the double boiler or the bowl from the hot water. Add the remaining 8 ounces of semisweet chocolate and stir until all of the chocolate is melted and smooth.

4· Insert a candy thermometer or chocolate thermometer into the melted chocolate. Its temperature should be 88 to 90°F. If the chocolate is too cold, place it back over the hot water until the temperature reaches 88 to 90°F. If it is too hot, let it cool until the desired temperature is reached.

5· Hold the strawberries by the stems and dip them into the chocolate up to the stem. Set them on the prepared cookie sheet. If the chocolate gets too shallow to dip all the strawberries, use a 1-inch pastry brush to paint the berries with chocolate or use a tablespoon to drizzle the chocolate over them. Place the strawberries in the refrigerator to allow the chocolate to harden, about 30 minutes.

6· When the chocolate on the strawberries is set, peel them off the wax paper. Store them in one layer in an airtight container in the refrigerator for up to 1 week.

VARIATIONS

MILK CHOCOLATE STRAWBERRIES Substitute 16 ounces milk chocolate for the semi-sweet chocolate.

WHITE CHOCOLATE STRAWBERRIES Substitute 16 ounces white chocolate for the semisweet chocolate.

These variations work with the base recipe or with either of the preceding chocolate variations.

CHOCOLATE BANANAS Substitute 24 1-inch peeled banana slices for the strawberries. Insert a toothpick into each piece of banana to dip it into the chocolate. Cover the fruit completely in chocolate. Remove the toothpick before the chocolate sets.

CHOCOLATE GOOSEBERRIES Substitute 36 large gooseberries for the strawberries. Peel the paper covering from the gooseberries to reveal the fruit. Hold the berries by the papery husks to dip them into the chocolate. Dip each one up to the husk.

CHOCOLATE GRAPES Substitute 36 large green grapes for the strawberries. Insert a toothpick into each grape to dip into the chocolate. Cover the fruit completely in chocolate. Remove the toothpick before the chocolate sets.

CHOCOLATE ORANGES Substitute 24 fresh orange sections for the strawberries. Use a pair of clean tweezers to dip the orange sections into the chocolate. Cover the fruit completely with chocolate.

CHOCOLATE LEAVES

Chocolate leaves are an easy-to-make decoration. On top of a cake, or as a garnish for ice cream or fruit salad, they'll dress up your desserts. Or they can be served as candy on their own. I use plastic leaves, which are not candy molds but plastic replicas of real leaves, complete with veins. They are made specifically for chocolate and you can find them at specialty cookware stores, or consult the Source Guide on page 242. You can use fresh leaves as long as they are nontoxic, clean, and pesticide-free. But always check with your county extension agent to be sure.

> 24 plastic leaves designed for candy making
>
> 8 ounces semisweet chocolate, coarsely chopped, *or* 8 ounces semisweet chocolate chips
>
> Butter or margarine for greasing the cookie sheet

1· Wash and dry the leaves. Butter a large cookie sheet and line it with wax paper. Set aside.

2· Melt 4 ounces of the semisweet chocolate in the top of a double boiler set over hot water. If you don't have a double boiler, simply place the chocolate in a bowl that fits snugly over a pot of hot water.

3· When the chocolate has melted completely, remove the top part of the double boiler or the bowl from the hot water. Add the remaining 4 ounces of semisweet chocolate and stir until all of the chocolate is melted and smooth.

4· Insert a candy thermometer or chocolate thermometer into the melted chocolate. Its temperature should be 88 to 90°F. If the chocolate is too cold, place it back over the hot water until the temperature reaches 88 to 90°F. If it is too hot, let it cool until the desired temperature is reached.

5· Using a ½-inch pastry brush, paint the leaves with the melted chocolate. Use the underside of fresh leaves for a realistic look with veins and stems. Plastic candy-making leaves are usually veined on the top for ease of use.

6· Set each leaf, chocolate side up, on the prepared cookie sheet. Set aside to allow the chocolate to harden, about 4 hours. The cooler your room's temperature, the faster the chocolate will harden. You can speed up the process by first placing the painted leaves in the refrigerator for 10 minutes, but no longer.

7· Once the chocolate is set, peel the plastic or fresh leaves away and store the chocolate leaves in one layer in an airtight container at room temperature for up to 2 weeks.

VARIATIONS

CHOCOLATE AUTUMN LEAVES Substitute 8 ounces white chocolate for the semisweet chocolate. Add 2 to 3 drops red, yellow, gold, or orange food coloring to the melted white chocolate before painting the leaves.

CHOCOLATE BAY LEAVES Use fresh bay leaves instead of plastic leaves. The natural oil from the bay leaf will flavor the chocolate, giving a mild herbal taste to the candy leaf.

CHOCOLATE GOLD LEAVES Lay a piece of edible gold leaf on top of each finished chocolate leaf. (To find gold leaf, consult the Source Guide, page 242.)

CHOCOLATE SILVER LEAVES Lay a piece of edible silver leaf on top of each finished chocolate leaf. (To find silver leaf, check the Source Guide, page 242.)

MILK CHOCOLATE LEAVES Substitute 8 ounces milk chocolate for the semisweet chocolate.

WHITE CHOCOLATE LEAVES Substitute 8 ounces white chocolate for the semisweet chocolate.

CHOCOLATE LOLLIPOPS

Lollipop molds are necessary for this recipe. They come in endless shapes and sizes—flowers, animals, geometrics, and sports figures. In fact, if you can name it, chances are there's a mold for it. Molds have a slot for the lollipop stick and a deep indentation at the end of the slot for the chocolate. When you fill the molds, it is important not to pour the chocolate into the slot meant for the stick. You also will need small bags for wrapping each finished pop. Bags come in many sizes. You will need to buy bags that fit around the lollipop shape you've chosen. Molds, sticks, and bags can be found in some kitchenware stores, or consult the Source Guide on page 242.

> 16 ounces milk chocolate, coarsely chopped, or 16 ounces milk chocolate chips
>
> 12 lollipop molds
>
> 12 lollipop sticks
>
> 12 small plastic bags, size determined by the mold
>
> Twelve 6-inch-long pieces ribbon

1· Melt 8 ounces of the milk chocolate in the top of a double boiler set over hot water. If you don't have a double boiler, simply place the chocolate in a bowl that fits snugly over a pot of hot water.

2· When the chocolate has melted completely, remove the top part of the double boiler or the bowl from the hot water. Add the remaining 8 ounces of milk chocolate and stir until all of the chocolate is melted and smooth.

3· Insert a candy thermometer or chocolate thermometer into the melted chocolate. Its temperature should be 86 to 88°F. If the chocolate is too cold, place it back over the hot water until the temperature reaches 86 to 88°F. If it is too hot, let it cool until the desired temperature is reached.

4· Pour the melted chocolate into the molds, making sure to leave the slot for the stick empty. Lay the stick into this slot so that ½ inch to ¾ inch of the stick is covered with chocolate.

5· Allow the molds to sit at room temperature for 6 hours or until the chocolate is completely firm. The cooler your room's temperature, the faster the chocolate will set. You can speed up this process by placing the molds in the refrigerator for 15 minutes, then allowing them to continue cooling at room temperature.

6· Peel or pop the lollipops from the molds and wrap each one in its own little plastic bag. Tie the bag closed with a piece of ribbon. Alternatively, store the lollipops in layers separated by wax paper in an airtight container at room temperature for up to 1 month.

VARIATIONS

CHOCOLATE CHRISTMAS LOLLIPOPS Use Christmas molds, such as angels, trees, Santas, wreaths, snowflakes, bells, or stockings. If desired, substitute 16 ounces white chocolate for the milk chocolate and add 3 drops of red or green food coloring to the melted white chocolate before pouring it into the molds.

CHOCOLATE CRUNCH LOLLIPOPS Place a few small crunchy candies such as M&M's or red hots into each mold before pouring in the melted chocolate.

CHOCOLATE EASTER LOLLIPOPS Use bunny-shaped molds. If desired, substitute 16 ounces white chocolate for the milk chocolate.

CHOCOLATE HALLOWEEN LOLLIPOPS Use Halloween-shaped molds such as pumpkins, bats, or witches. If desired, substitute 16 ounces white chocolate for the milk chocolate. Add 2 to 3 drops of orange or black food coloring to the melted white chocolate before pouring it into the molds.

CHOCOLATE HANUKKAH LOLLIPOPS Use Hanukkah molds such as dreidels or menorahs. If desired, substitute 16 ounces white chocolate for the milk chocolate and add 3 drops of blue food coloring to the melted white chocolate before pouring it into the molds.

CHOCOLATE SPRING LOLLIPOPS Use flower molds, substituting 16 ounces white chocolate for the milk chocolate. Add 2 to 3 drops of pastel food coloring to the melted white chocolate before pouring into the molds. If desired, divide the melted chocolate into 2 or 3 small bowls and use a different color in each. You will have a colorful garden of flower lollipops.

CHOCOLATE VALENTINE'S LOLLIPOPS Use heart-shaped or rose-shaped molds. If desired, substitute 16 ounces white chocolate for the milk chocolate and add 3 drops of red or pink food coloring to the melted white chocolate before pouring it into the molds.

FLAVORED CHOCOLATE LOLLIPOPS Add ½ teaspoon almond, lemon, orange, banana, maple, or rum extract to the melted chocolate before pouring it into the molds.

CHOCOLATE MATZO

At the Jewish holiday of Passover, matzo, a crispy, flat, unleavened bread, is eaten for eight days. It usually comes in two varieties: plain and egg. Either can be used for this recipe. Chocolate matzo is just perfect for dessert, along with fresh fruit and a cup of hot coffee or tea.

> 24 ounces semisweet chocolate, coarsely chopped, or 24 ounces semisweet chocolate chips
>
> One 1-pound box square matzo

1· Melt 12 ounces of the semisweet chocolate in the top of a double boiler set over hot water. If you don't have a double boiler, simply place the chocolate in a bowl that fits snugly over a pot of hot water.

2· When the chocolate has melted completely, remove the top part of the double boiler or the bowl from the hot water. Add the remaining 12 ounces of semisweet chocolate and stir until all of the chocolate is melted and smooth.

3· Insert a candy thermometer or chocolate thermometer into the melted chocolate. Its temperature should be 88 to 90°F. If the chocolate is too cold, place it back over the hot water until the temperature reaches 88 to 90°F. If it is too hot, let it cool until the desired temperature is reached.

4· Use a 2-inch pastry brush to paint one side of each piece of matzo with the melted chocolate. Set aside, chocolate side up, at room temperature, until the chocolate has hardened, about 4 hours. The cooler your room's temperature, the faster the chocolate will harden. You can speed up the process by first placing the painted matzo in the refrigerator for 10 minutes, but no longer.

5· With your hands, break each matzo into 4 pieces. Store them in an airtight container at room temperature for up to 2 weeks.

VARIATIONS

MILK CHOCOLATE MATZO Substitute 24 ounces milk chocolate for the semisweet chocolate.

WHITE CHOCOLATE MATZO Substitute 24 ounces white chocolate for the semisweet chocolate.

The following variations work with the base recipe or with either of the preceding chocolate variations.

COCONUT CHOCOLATE MATZO Immediately after brushing the matzo with the chocolate, sprinkle each with 2 tablespoons toasted, shredded coconut (for advice on toasting coconut, see page 12).

JACKSON POLLOCK CHOCOLATE MATZO Once the semisweet chocolate has set, drizzle each matzo with 2 tablespoons of any of the following: melted white chocolate, melted milk chocolate, melted butterscotch chips, or melted caramels. Let the kids have fun creating their own works of art on these matzo canvases.

JEWISH S'MORES Reduce the amount of chocolate to 12 ounces. When all the chocolate is used up, use a knife to spread the remaining pieces of matzo with a ¼-inch layer of purchased marshmallow cream. Create S'mores by sandwiching one piece of chocolate matzo and one piece of marshmallow matzo, coated sides together.

PEANUT BUTTER CHOCOLATE MATZO Spread each matzo with a ⅛- to ¼-inch layer of creamy peanut butter and set it in the freezer for 2 hours before brushing it with the melted chocolate.

PEANUT CHOCOLATE MATZO Immediately after brushing the matzo with the chocolate, sprinkle each with 2 tablespoons chopped salted peanuts.

CHOCOLATE PIZZA

This sweet gives new meaning to the notion of a pizza party. The crust tastes just like a giant candy bar, colored peanut butter takes the place of tomato sauce, and grated white chocolate makes terrific cheese. Check the variations for additional topping ideas, or let your kids come up with their own. Just hold the anchovies.

> 32 ounces semisweet chocolate, coarsely chopped, or 32 ounces semisweet chocolate chips
>
> 2 cups crushed Frosted Flakes cereal
>
> 6 to 7 drops red food coloring
>
> 1 cup smooth peanut butter
>
> ½ cup golden raisins
>
> ½ cup chocolate chips
>
> 8 ounces white chocolate, grated
>
> Butter or margarine for greasing the cookie sheet

1· Butter a large cookie sheet and line it with wax paper. Set it aside.

2· Melt 16 ounces of the semisweet chocolate in the top of a double boiler set over hot water. If you don't have a double boiler, simply place the chocolate in a bowl that fits snugly over a pot of hot water.

3· When the chocolate has melted completely, remove the top part of the double boiler or the bowl from the hot water. Add the remaining 16 ounces of semisweet chocolate and stir until all of the chocolate is melted and smooth.

4· Insert a candy thermometer or chocolate thermometer into the melted chocolate. Its temperature should be 88 to 90°F. If the chocolate is too cold, place it back over the hot water until the temperature reaches 88 to 90°F. If it is too hot, let it cool until the desired temperature is reached.

5· Add the cereal flakes and stir with a wooden spoon until the mixture is thoroughly combined.

6· To make the "crust," spread the mixture into a 16-inch circle on the prepared cookie sheet. Score the top with a knife into at least 12 slices, going all the way to the edge.

7· Blend 6 to 7 drops red food coloring into the peanut butter to make it look like tomato sauce. Spread the colored peanut butter over the hardened chocolate crust, leaving a ¼-inch edge all the way around. Sprinkle the raisins and chips over the peanut butter and lightly press them down to set them in place. Sprinkle the grated white chocolate over the top to resemble cheese.

8· Break or cut the pizza along the scored lines. Store the pieces in layers, separated by wax paper, in an airtight container in the refrigerator for up to 1 week.

CANDY PIZZA TOPPINGS Substitute any combination of the following for the raisins and chocolate chips to make 1 cup of topping.

Banana chips

Candied cherries (red or green)

Candy corn

Caramel corn

Chocolate-covered peanuts

Chocolate-covered raisins

Chopped almonds

Chopped dried apricots

Chopped dried dates

Chopped dried figs

Chopped pecans

Chopped walnuts

Crumbled candy bars

Crumbled potato chips

Dried apple rings

Granola

Gummy bears

Gummy frogs

Gummy worms

Jordan almonds

M&M's candies (plain, peanut, almond, or crispy)

Pignoli nuts

Shelled pistachios

CHOCOLATE POTATO CHIPS

I've seen these selling for lots of money at candy shops and fudge factories in tony resort towns. Now you can make your own.

> 24 ounces semisweet chocolate, coarsely chopped, or 24 ounces semisweet chocolate chips
>
> One 16-ounce bag plain Ruffles potato chips
>
> Butter or margarine for greasing the cookie sheet

1· Butter a large cookie sheet and line it with wax paper. Set aside.

2· Melt 12 ounces of the semisweet chocolate in the top of a double boiler set over hot water. If you don't have a double boiler, simply place the chocolate in a bowl that fits snugly over a pot of hot water.

3· When the chocolate has melted completely, remove the top part of the double boiler or the bowl from the hot water. Add the remaining 12 ounces of semisweet chocolate and stir until all of the chocolate is melted and smooth.

4· Insert a candy thermometer or chocolate thermometer into the melted chocolate. Its temperature should be 88 to 90°F. If the chocolate is too cold, place it back over the hot water until the temperature reaches 88 to 90°F. If it is too hot, let it cool until the desired temperature is reached.

5· Using a 1-inch pastry brush, paint one side of each potato chip with ⅛ inch to ¼ inch of the melted chocolate. Depending on how thick you paint the chocolate on the chips, you may or may not use the entire bag of chips.

6· Place the painted chips on the prepared cookie sheet, chocolate side up. Set aside at room temperature until the chocolate is set and hard, about 4 hours. The cooler your room's temperature, the faster the chocolate will harden. You can speed up the process by first placing the chips in the refrigerator for 10 minutes, but no longer.

7· Store the chips in an airtight container at room temperature for up to 1 week.

VARIATIONS

BUTTERSCOTCH POTATO CHIPS Substitute 24 ounces butterscotch chips for the semi-sweet chocolate.

MILK CHOCOLATE POTATO CHIPS Substitute 24 ounces milk chocolate for the semi-sweet chocolate.

WHITE CHOCOLATE POTATO CHIPS Substitute 24 ounces white chocolate for the semisweet chocolate.

The following variations work with the base recipe or with any of the preceding variations.

BIRTHDAY PARTY CHOCOLATE POTATO CHIPS Immediately after brushing each chip with the melted chocolate, sprinkle it with 1 teaspoon colorful sprinkles or sparkling colored sugar.

CANDY CHOCOLATE POTATO CHIPS Immediately after brushing each chip with the melted chocolate, sprinkle it with a few small candies of your choice, such as M&M's, Raisinets, Goobers, or red hots.

CHOCOLATE VINEGAR POTATO CHIPS Substitute vinegar-and-salt–flavor potato chips for the plain potato chips.

CRANBERRY CHOCOLATE POTATO CHIPS Immediately after brushing each chip with the melted chocolate, sprinkle it with a few whole dried cranberries.

DIPPED CHOCOLATE POTATO CHIPS Instead of painting one side of the chips with a pastry brush, simply dip each chip into the melted chocolate halfway.

DOUBLE-DIPPED CHOCOLATE POTATO CHIPS Instead of painting one side of the chips with a pastry brush, simply dip each chip into the melted chocolate halfway. Once the chocolate is set, dip the plain half into melted white chocolate, following the same technique for melting the chocolate.

NUTTY CHOCOLATE POTATO CHIPS Immediately after brushing each chip with melted chocolate, sprinkle with 1 teaspoon of any chopped nuts: peanuts, almonds, hazelnuts, walnuts, or pecans.

CHOCOLATE PRETZELS

While pretzels come in many shapes and sizes, long pretzel logs are the easiest to dip. Once dipped, they are sweet, salty, and crunchy—a great treat for kids or your friends.

> 24 ounces milk chocolate, coarsely chopped, or 24 ounces milk chocolate chips
>
> 24 pretzel logs
>
> Butter or margarine for greasing the cookie sheet

1· Butter a large cookie sheet and line it with wax paper. Set aside.

2· Melt 12 ounces of the milk chocolate in the top of a double boiler set over hot water. If you don't have a double boiler, simply place the chocolate in a bowl that fits snugly over a pot of hot water.

3· When the chocolate has melted completely, remove the top part of the double boiler or the bowl from the hot water. Add the remaining 12 ounces of milk chocolate and stir until all of the chocolate is melted and smooth.

4· Insert a candy thermometer or chocolate thermometer into the melted chocolate. Its temperature should be 86 to 88°F. If the chocolate is too cold, place it back over the hot water until the temperature reaches 86 to 88°F. If it is too hot, let it cool until the desired temperature is reached.

5· Pour the melted chocolate into a tall, thin glass, leaving a 1-inch space at the top. Dip each pretzel into the chocolate at least halfway up (keep adding more melted chocolate to the glass as the level goes down). Place the dipped pretzels on the prepared cookie sheet. Set aside, at room temperature, until the chocolate is set and hard, about 4 hours. The cooler your room's temperature, the faster the chocolate will harden. You can speed up the process by first placing the dipped pretzels in the refrigerator for 20 minutes, but no longer.

6· Store the pretzels in layers, separated by wax paper, in an airtight container at room temperature for up to 2 weeks.

VARIATIONS

SEMISWEET CHOCOLATE PRETZELS Substitute 24 ounces semisweet chocolate for the milk chocolate.

WHITE CHOCOLATE PRETZELS Substitute 24 ounces white chocolate for the milk chocolate.

The following variations work with the base recipe or with either of the preceding chocolate variations.

CHOCOLATE CARAMEL PRETZELS Melt 24 store-bought caramels in a small bowl set over simmering water. Drizzle melted caramel over the dipped pretzel logs on the wax paper.

CHOCOLATE COCONUT PRETZELS Immediately after laying the pretzels on the wax paper, sprinkle the pretzels with 1 cup shredded, sweetened coconut.

CHOCOLATE NUTTY PRETZELS Immediately after laying the pretzels on the wax paper, sprinkle the pretzels with 1 cup chopped peanuts, hazelnuts, cashews, or almonds.

CHOCOLATE PEANUT BUTTER PRETZELS Spread a thin layer (⅛ inch) of peanut butter halfway up each pretzel log before dipping them into the melted chocolate. Make sure the chocolate completely covers the peanut butter.

EVERYTHING PRETZELS Immediately after dipping the pretzels and laying them on wax paper, sprinkle with ⅓ cup shredded, sweetened coconut, ⅓ cup chopped nuts, and ⅓ cup butterscotch chips. Drizzle with 24 melted store-bought caramels and allow everything to set and harden before removing the pretzels from the wax paper, about 4 hours.

CHOCOLATE SPIDERWEBS

MAKES 4 TO 6 SPIDERWEBS, DEPENDING ON SIZE

The perfect treat for Halloween, these chocolate webs make unique party favors. You can also use small webs to decorate a scoop of ice cream, or lay one large web on top of a ghoulish cake.

> 12 ounces white chocolate, coarsely chopped, or 12 ounces white chocolate chips
>
> Butter or margarine for greasing the cookie sheet

1· Butter a large cookie sheet and set it aside.

2· Cut a piece of parchment paper large enough to fit the cookie sheet. Using a dark pencil or a magic marker, draw spiderweb designs, about 6 inches in diameter, onto the parchment, leaving 2 to 3 inches between each web. Turn the paper over and place it onto the prepared cookie sheet. You should be able to see your design through the parchment.

3· Melt 6 ounces of the white chocolate in the top of a double boiler set over hot water. If you don't have a double boiler, simply place the chocolate in a bowl that fits snugly over a pot of hot water.

4· When the chocolate has melted completely, remove the top part of the double boiler or the bowl from the hot water. Add the remaining 6 ounces white chocolate and stir until all of the chocolate is melted and smooth.

5· Insert a candy thermometer or chocolate thermometer into the melted chocolate. Its temperature should be 86 to 88°F. If the chocolate is too cold, place it back over the hot water until the temperature reaches 86 to 88°F. If it is too hot, let it cool until the desired temperature is reached.

6· Fill a large Ziploc bag with the melted chocolate. Seal the bag and use a pair of scissors to cut the tip off one bottom corner. The hole should be about ¼ inch. If desired, use a pastry bag fitted with a ¼-inch round tip.

7. Squeezing the bag, follow the design you drew on the parchment paper, making the lines thick enough to hold together when the chocolate hardens, at least ¼ inch.

8. Place the webs in the refrigerator for about 1 hour or until they have hardened. Carefully peel the webs off the parchment. Store them in layers, separated by wax paper, in an airtight container at room temperature or in the refrigerator for up to 2 weeks.

VARIATIONS

CHRISTMAS SPIDERWEBS Sprinkle each web with 2 to 3 teaspoons red and green sprinkles while the chocolate is still soft.

DUSTY SPIDERWEBS Sift 2 teaspoons cocoa powder over the finished spiderwebs.

FROSTED SPIDERWEBS Sprinkle each web with 1 to 2 teaspoons superfine sugar before placing them in the refrigerator to harden.

HALLOWEEN SPIDERWEBS Sprinkle each web with 2 teaspoons orange and black sprinkles while the chocolate is still soft.

MILK CHOCOLATE SPIDERWEBS Substitute 12 ounces milk chocolate for the white chocolate.

SEMISWEET SPIDERWEBS Substitute 12 ounces semisweet chocolate for the white chocolate.

SPIDERWEBS WITH SPIDERS Place a gummy spider into the middle of each web while the chocolate is still soft.

COCONUT HAYSTACKS

MAKES ABOUT 1 POUND

Although the white chocolate chips available in your supermarket will work well in this recipe, these smooth and crunchy candies are best made with the finest white chocolate you can afford.

> 1 heaping cup shredded, sweetened coconut
>
> 10 ounces white chocolate, coarsely chopped, or 10 ounces white chocolate chips
>
> Butter or margarine for greasing the cookie sheet

1· Butter a large cookie sheet and line it with wax paper. Set aside. Preheat the oven to 350°F.

2· Spread the coconut on a baking sheet and place in the preheated oven for 5 to 7 minutes or until lightly toasted. Toss the coconut once or twice during baking to ensure even browning. Be careful not to let it burn. Transfer the coconut to a bowl to cool completely.

3· Melt 5 ounces of the white chocolate in the top of a double boiler set over hot water. If you don't have a double boiler, simply place the chocolate in a bowl that fits snugly over a pot of hot water.

4· When the chocolate has melted completely, remove the top part of the double boiler or the bowl from the hot water. Add the remaining 5 ounces of white chocolate and stir until all of the chocolate is melted and smooth.

5· Insert a candy thermometer or chocolate thermometer into the melted chocolate. Its temperature should be 86 to 88°F. If the chocolate is too cold, place it back over the hot water until the temperature reaches 86 to 88°F. If it is too hot, let it cool until the desired temperature is reached.

6· Add the cooled, toasted coconut all at once to the melted chocolate and mix with a wooden spoon until thoroughly combined.

7· Drop tablespoonsful of the chocolate coconut mixture onto the prepared cookie sheet, creating tall haystacks. Allow the stacks to harden at room temperature, about 4 hours, or place them in the refrigerator for 1 hour.

8· Store the haystacks in one layer in an airtight container at room temperature or in the refrigerator for up to 3 weeks.

VARIATIONS

BUTTERSCOTCH COCONUT HAYSTACKS Substitute 10 ounces butterscotch chips for the white chocolate.

MILK CHOCOLATE COCONUT HAYSTACKS Substitute 10 ounces milk chocolate for the white chocolate.

SEMISWEET CHOCOLATE COCONUT HAYSTACKS Substitute 10 ounces semisweet chocolate for the white chocolate.

The following variations work with the base recipe or with any of the preceding variations.

CHERRY COCONUT HAYSTACKS Add ½ cup chopped candied cherries with the coconut to the melted chocolate.

CHEWY COCONUT HAYSTACKS Use untoasted, shredded sweetened coconut.

COCONUT CUPS Add the coconut to the chocolate and immediately drop tablespoonsful of the mixture into small paper candy cups. The chocolate will cool and set up in the cups. To eat, simply peel away the paper.

SUNFLOWER COCONUT HAYSTACKS Add ½ cup shelled sunflower seeds with the coconut to the melted chocolate.

COCONUT SNOWBALLS

These candies belong in the freezer, right next to your Girl Scout thin mints and your Snickers bars. They have crispy coconut on the outside and sweet chewy coconut on the inside. They're sure to become another one of your all-time favorite frozen treats.

> 5 cups sweetened, shredded coconut
>
> One 14-ounce can sweetened condensed milk (regular, low-fat, or nonfat)
>
> ⅓ cup light corn syrup
>
> 1 tablespoon vanilla extract
>
> 1 pound confectioners' sugar

1· Preheat the oven to 350°F.

2· Spread 2 cups of the coconut on a baking sheet and place in the preheated oven for 5 to 7 minutes, or until lightly toasted. Toss the coconut once or twice during baking to ensure even browning. Be careful not to let it burn. Transfer the coconut to a bowl to cool completely.

3· In a large mixing bowl, combine the remaining 3 cups coconut, the sweetened condensed milk, corn syrup, and vanilla. Beat by hand or with an electric mixer until well blended. Slowly add the confectioners' sugar and beat for 2 more minutes. Place in the refrigerator until cold.

4· With your hands, form the chilled mixture into 1-inch balls. Roll each one in the toasted coconut. Make sure each ball is generously coated. Place them on a large platter in the freezer for at least 1 hour before serving.

5· Store the snowballs in an airtight container in the freezer for up to 1 month.

VARIATIONS

ALMOND COCONUT SNOWBALLS Reduce the amount of coconut to 3 cups. Omit toasting the coconut. Roll the finished balls in 2 cups toasted, sliced almonds. For advice on toasting nuts, see page 12.

CHOCOLATE COCONUT SNOWBALLS Substitute chocolate-flavored sweetened condensed milk for the sweetened condensed milk.

CHRISTMAS COCONUT SNOWBALLS Add ¼ cup each chopped red and green candied cherries to the mixture before adding the sugar.

KEY LIME PIE COCONUT SNOWBALLS Add 2 tablespoons lime juice, 1 teaspoon grated fresh lime rind, and ½ cup graham cracker crumbs to the coconut mixture before adding the confectioners' sugar.

PIÑA COLADA SNOWBALLS Substitute artificial rum flavoring for the vanilla and add ½ cup coarsely chopped dried pineapple to the coconut mixture before adding the sugar.

CREAM CHEESE MINTS

These old-fashioned candies were an everyday treat in farmhouses across the upper Midwest. Don't use fat-free cream cheese because the texture is not thick enough to allow the candies to hold their shape. They can be shaped by hand or with candy molds (check your local kitchenware store or see the Source Guide, page 242).

> 3 ounces cream cheese, at room temperature
>
> 2½ to 3 cups confectioners' sugar
>
> ½ teaspoon mint extract or 4 to 6 drops peppermint oil
>
> 6 drops green food coloring
>
> 1 cup superfine sugar for coating

1· In a medium mixing bowl, beat the cream cheese until softened. Slowly add 1½ cups of the confectioners' sugar. Beat in the mint extract and food coloring until well blended. Add the remaining confectioners' sugar ¼ cup at a time until a soft dough is formed.

2· Turn onto a counter or board dusted with confectioners' sugar and knead the dough for 5 minutes. (Add more confectioners' sugar, 1 tablespoon at a time, if the dough is too soft and sticky.)

3· With your hands, roll tablespoonsful of the dough into balls, then roll each ball into superfine sugar. Flatten the balls slightly into patties.

4· The sugared mint balls can also be pressed into candy molds. The coating of superfine sugar will allow them to release easily from the molds. Adjust the amount of dough used for each mint according to the shape and size of the mold you choose.

5· Store the mints in layers, separated by wax paper, in an airtight container in the refrigerator for up to 2 weeks.

VARIATIONS

CHOCOLATE CREAM CHEESE MINTS Omit the food coloring. Substitute 1 cup cocoa powder for 1 cup of the confectioners' sugar.

CHRISTMAS CREAM CHEESE MINTS Substitute red food coloring for the green food coloring if desired. Press the mints into Christmas molds such as Santas, snowflakes, sleighs, snowmen, Christmas trees, or angels after coating with superfine sugar.

EASTER CREAM CHEESE MINTS Substitute pastel pink, yellow, or blue food coloring for the green food coloring. Press the mints into Easter molds such as bunnies, eggs, baskets, or flowers after coating with superfine sugar.

HALLOWEEN CREAM CHEESE MINTS Substitute orange or black coloring for the green food coloring. Shape into flat patties or press mints into pumpkin, bat, or witch molds after rolling the mints in the superfine sugar.

HANUKKAH CREAM CHEESE MINTS Substitute blue food coloring for the green food coloring or omit the food coloring altogether. Press the mints into Hanukkah molds such as menorahs and dreidels after coating with superfine sugar.

HERBAL CREAM CHEESE CANDIES Add 2 tablespoons finely chopped fresh herbs such as basil, tarragon, thyme, or marjoram with the mint.

LEMON CREAM CHEESE CANDIES Substitute 1 teaspoon lemon extract for the mint extract and yellow food coloring for the green.

LOWER-FAT CREAM CHEESE MINTS Substitute 3 ounces reduced-fat cream cheese for the regular cream cheese. Do not use fat-free cream cheese as it doesn't hold its shape.

RUM CREAM CHEESE CANDIES Substitute 1 teaspoon artificial rum flavoring for the mint extract and omit the food coloring.

VALENTINE'S CREAM CHEESE MINTS Substitute red food coloring for the green food coloring. Shape the mints into hearts after coating with superfine sugar or press them into heart-shaped molds.

CRISPY RICE CEREAL BARK

Crunchy Rice Krispies and smooth milk chocolate give this bark the same texture as Nestlé's Crunch bars.

> 12 ounces milk chocolate, coarsely chopped, or 12 ounces milk chocolate chips
>
> 3 cups Rice Krispies cereal
>
> Butter or margarine for greasing the cookie sheet

1· Butter a large cookie sheet and line it with wax paper.

2· Melt 6 ounces of the milk chocolate in the top of a double boiler set over hot water. If you don't have a double boiler, simply place the chocolate in a bowl that fits snugly over a pot of hot water.

3· When the chocolate has melted completely, remove the top part of the double boiler or the bowl from the hot water. Add the remaining 6 ounces of milk chocolate and stir until all of the chocolate is melted and smooth.

4· Insert a candy thermometer or chocolate thermometer into the melted chocolate. Its temperature should be 86 to 88°F. If the chocolate is too cold, place it back over the hot water until the temperature reaches 86 to 88°F. If it is too hot, let it cool until the desired temperature is reached.

5· Add the cereal all at once and stir with a wooden spoon until completely blended.

6· Pour the chocolate mixture onto the prepared cookie sheet and spread it with a spatula or wooden spoon to about a ½-inch thickness. Don't worry if the chocolate doesn't reach the sides and corners of the cookie sheet; a free-form shape is preferred.

7· Let the bark set up and harden at room temperature, about 4 hours. The cooler your room's temperature, the faster the bark will harden. You can speed up the process by first placing the bark in the refrigerator for 10 minutes, but no longer.

8· Grab the edges of the cooled bark and peel it off the wax paper in one piece, if possible. Break it with your hands into irregular pieces, about the size of a credit card. Store the candy in an airtight container at room temperature for up to 1 month.

VARIATIONS

SEMISWEET CRISPY RICE CEREAL BARK Substitute 12 ounces semisweet chocolate for the milk chocolate.

WHITE CRISPY RICE CEREAL BARK Substitute 12 ounces white chocolate for the milk chocolate.

The following variations work with the base recipe or with either of the preceding chocolate variations.

BANANA CRISPY RICE CEREAL BARK Add ¼ cup lightly crumbled dried banana chips with the cereal to the melted chocolate.

BLUEBERRY CRISPY RICE CEREAL BARK Add ¼ cup whole dried blueberries with the cereal to the melted chocolate.

CINNAMON CRISPY RICE CEREAL BARK Add ½ teaspoon ground cinnamon with the cereal to the melted chocolate.

CRANBERRY CRISPY RICE CEREAL BARK Add ¼ cup whole dried cranberries with the cereal to the melted chocolate.

MARSHMALLOW CRISPY RICE CEREAL BARK Add ⅓ cup miniature marshmallows with the cereal to the melted chocolate.

RAISIN CRISPY RICE CEREAL BARK Add ¼ cup whole raisins (dark or golden) with the cereal to the melted chocolate.

WALNUT CRISPY RICE CEREAL BARK Add ¼ cup coarsely chopped walnuts with the cereal to the melted chocolate.

FRUIT BALLS

These treats are chewy and full of natural energy. The texture reminds me of the center of Fig Newtons. You'll need to grind the dried fruit to make this candy smooth. If you don't have a meat grinder, you can use a food mill. Do not use a food processor; it will only chop the mixture, leaving small chunks.

> 1 small tangerine (or orange)
> 1½ cups dark raisins
> 1 cup dried, pitted dates
> 1 cup dried figs
> ½ cup pitted prunes
> ¾ cup finely chopped walnuts
> 1 cup confectioners' sugar, for coating

1· Peel the tangerine (or orange) and, using a sharp knife, remove as much of the white pith from under the peel as you can. Finely mince the peel or "zest" and set aside.

2· Squeeze the juice from the fruit membranes into a small bowl and set that aside. Discard what remains of the fruit.

3· Grind the raisins, dates, figs, prunes, and tangerine zest in a meat grinder fitted with a fine blade, or in a food mill. Stir in the reserved juice and the chopped walnuts.

4· Let the mixture rest in the refrigerator overnight.

5· Roll the mixture into 1-inch balls with your hands. Roll each ball in confectioners' sugar. Store them in an airtight container in layers, separated by wax paper, at room temperature for up to 1 week.

VARIATIONS

APRICOT PISTACHIO FRUIT BALLS Substitute 1 cup coarsely chopped dried apricots for the dates and ½ cup shelled pistachios for the walnuts.

CHERRY ALMOND FRUIT BALLS Substitute 1 cup whole dried cherries for the raisins and ½ cup slivered almonds for the walnuts.

CRANBERRY PECAN FRUIT BALLS Substitute 1 cup whole dried cranberries for the raisins and ½ cup pecan pieces for the walnuts.

SPICED FRUIT BALLS Add ½ teaspoon ground cinnamon, ½ teaspoon ground ginger, ¼ teaspoon ground nutmeg, and ¼ teaspoon ground cloves with the juice and nuts.

FUDGE-IN-A-MINUTE

No one will ever guess that this creamy fudge is made with only three ingredients, or that it takes just a few minutes to prepare.

> 16 ounces semisweet chocolate chips
>
> 3 tablespoons unsalted butter plus additional for greasing the pan
>
> One 14-ounce can sweetened condensed milk (regular, low-fat, or nonfat)

1· Line an 8-inch square pan with wax paper. The paper should overlap the pan by 2 inches on all sides. Butter the wax paper and set the pan aside.

2· Melt the chocolate and butter together in a small, heavy pan over very low heat. Stir constantly to avoid burning the chocolate. When the chocolate is melted, remove the pan from the heat and stir in the sweetened condensed milk. Stir with a wooden spoon until the mixture is blended to a uniform color and consistency. Pour the mixture into the prepared pan.

3· Place the pan in the refrigerator for 4 to 6 hours, or until set. When the fudge is firm, grab the edges of the wax paper and remove the fudge from the pan by lifting out the paper. Cut the fudge into squares. Store them in layers, separated by wax paper, in an airtight container in the refrigerator for up to 2 weeks.

VARIATIONS

BUTTERSCOTCH WALNUT FUDGE-IN-A-MINUTE Substitute 16 ounces butterscotch chips for the semisweet chocolate chips. Stir in 1 cup coarsely chopped walnuts with the sweetened condensed milk.

DARK CHOCOLATE MINT FUDGE-IN-A-MINUTE Add 1 teaspoon mint extract with the sweetened condensed milk. If desired, add ½ cup crushed peppermint candies at the same time.

DOUBLE CHOCOLATE FUDGE-IN-A-MINUTE Substitute chocolate-flavored sweetened condensed milk for the regular sweetened condensed milk.

FUDGE-IN-A-MINUTE NUT BALLS After cutting the fudge into squares, roll each square into a ball between your palms. Then roll each one in chopped nuts (your choice) to cover.

MARSHMALLOW ALMOND FUDGE-IN-A-MINUTE Add ¾ cup miniature marshmallows and ¾ cup toasted, sliced almonds after stirring in the sweetened condensed milk. (For advice on toasting nuts, see page 12.)

MILK CHOCOLATE FUDGE-IN-A-MINUTE Substitute 16 ounces milk chocolate chips for the semisweet chips.

GOLDEN RAISIN BARK

I imagine this light bark as coming from a birch tree—white, with flecks of gold. Use the sweetest, plumpest golden raisins you can find for this ethereal treat.

> 12 ounces white chocolate, coarsely chopped, or 12 ounces white chocolate chips
>
> ¾ cup golden raisins
>
> Butter or margarine for greasing the cookie sheet

1· Butter a large cookie sheet and line it with wax paper.

2· Melt 6 ounces of the white chocolate in the top of a double boiler set over hot water. If you don't have a double boiler, simply place the chocolate in a bowl that fits snugly over a pot of hot water.

3· When the chocolate has melted completely, remove the top part of the double boiler or the bowl from the hot water. Add the remaining 6 ounces of white chocolate and stir until all of the chocolate is melted and smooth.

4· Insert a candy thermometer or chocolate thermometer into the melted chocolate. Its temperature should be 86 to 88°F. If the chocolate is too cold, place it back over the hot water until the temperature reaches 86 to 88°F. If it is too hot, let it cool until the desired temperature is reached.

5· Add the raisins all at once and stir with a wooden spoon until the raisins are completely coated in chocolate.

6· Pour the chocolate mixture onto the prepared cookie sheet and spread it with a spatula or wooden spoon to about a ½-inch thickness. Don't worry if the chocolate doesn't reach the sides and corners of the cookie sheet; a free-form shape is preferred.

7· Let the bark set up and harden at room temperature, about 4 hours. The cooler your room's temperature, the faster the bark will harden. You can speed up the process by first placing the bark in the refrigerator for 10 minutes, but no longer.

8. Grab the edges of the cooled bark and peel it off the wax paper in one piece, if possible. Break it with your hands into irregular pieces, about the size of a credit card. Store the candy in an airtight container at room temperature for up to 1 month.

VARIATIONS

MILK CHOCOLATE RAISIN BARK Substitute 12 ounces milk chocolate for the white chocolate.

SEMISWEET RAISIN BARK Substitute 12 ounces semisweet chocolate for the white chocolate.

The following variations work with the base recipe or with either of the preceding chocolate variations.

CINNAMON RAISIN WALNUT BARK Add ¼ cup coarsely chopped walnuts and ¼ teaspoon ground cinnamon with the raisins to the melted chocolate.

DARK RAISIN BARK Substitute ¾ cup dark raisins for the golden raisins.

RAISIN PEANUT BARK Add ¼ cup coarsely chopped salted peanuts with the raisins to the melted chocolate.

RAISIN WALNUT BARK Add ¼ cup coarsely chopped walnuts with the raisins to the melted chocolate.

RUM RAISIN BARK Add 1 teaspoon artificial rum flavoring with the raisins to the melted chocolate.

GRANOLA DROPS

When I first decided to write a candy book, my agent Susan said she loved making simple treats for her kids, like chocolate mixed with granola. I turned that idea into these chewy, crunchy, creamy drops. Use any granola, store-bought or homemade.

> 16 ounces milk chocolate, coarsely chopped, or 16 ounces milk chocolate chips
>
> 1¼ cups granola cereal
>
> Butter or margarine for greasing the cookie sheet

1 · Butter a large cookie sheet and line it with wax paper. Set aside.

2 · Melt 8 ounces of the milk chocolate in the top of a double boiler set over hot water. If you don't have a double boiler, simply place the chocolate in a bowl that fits snugly over a pot of hot water.

3 · When the chocolate has melted completely, remove the top part of the double boiler or the bowl from the hot water. Add the remaining 8 ounces milk chocolate and stir until all of the chocolate is melted and smooth.

4 · Insert a candy thermometer or chocolate thermometer into the melted chocolate. Its temperature should be 86 to 88°F. If the chocolate is too cold, place it back over the hot water until the temperature reaches 86 to 88°F. If it is too hot, let it cool until the desired temperature is reached.

5 · Add the granola all at once and stir until the mixture is thoroughly combined.

6 · Drop tablespoonsful of the chocolate granola mixture onto the prepared cookie sheet and allow the drops to harden at room temperature, about 4 hours. The cooler your room's temperature, the faster the chocolate will harden. You can speed up the process by first placing them in the refrigerator for 10 minutes, but no longer.

7 · Store the granola drops in an airtight container at room temperature for up to 1 month.

VARIATIONS

DARK GRANOLA DROPS Substitute 16 ounces semisweet chocolate for the milk chocolate.

HONEY GRANOLA DROPS Add 2 tablespoons honey to the melted chocolate. Place the drops in the refrigerator to harden, about ½ hour.

WHITE GRANOLA DROPS Substitute 16 ounces white chocolate for the milk chocolate.

GRANOLA PEANUT BUTTER TRAIL BARS

It's easy to make these granola bars to pack in your briefcase or knapsack, for the office or the trail. Use your own homemade or store-bought granola.

> 1 cup light corn syrup
> ½ cup packed light brown sugar
> 1½ cups smooth peanut butter
> 1 cup powdered nonfat milk
> 2 teaspoons vanilla extract
> 3 cups granola cereal
> Vegetable oil for greasing the pan

1· Oil a 9 × 13-inch pan. Line the pan with wax paper, then lightly oil the paper and set the pan aside.

2· In a heavy medium saucepan, combine the corn syrup and brown sugar. Place over medium heat and stir until the sugar completely dissolves. Raise the heat to high and bring the mixture to a boil. Cook for 30 seconds.

3· Remove the pan from the heat and stir in the peanut butter, powdered milk, and vanilla. When the mixture is smooth, stir in the granola.

4· Spread the mixture into the prepared pan and place it in the refrigerator to cool. Cut the cooled mixture into bars and wrap each one in wax paper. Store them in an airtight container in the refrigerator for up to 1 week.

VARIATIONS

BLUEBERRY GRANOLA PEANUT BUTTER TRAIL BARS Reduce the amount of granola to 2 cups. Add 1 cup whole dried blueberries with the cereal.

CHERRY GRANOLA PEANUT BUTTER TRAIL BARS Reduce the amount of granola to 2 cups. Add 1 cup whole dried cherries with the cereal.

CHOCOLATE CHIP GRANOLA PEANUT BUTTER TRAIL BAR Add ¾ cup chocolate chips (milk, semisweet, white, or any combination that equals ¾ cup) with the granola.

MALTED MILK GRANOLA PEANUT BUTTER TRAIL BARS Reduce the amount of powdered milk to ¾ cup. Add ¼ cup malted milk powder with the remaining powdered milk.

POPCORN GRANOLA PEANUT BUTTER TRAIL BARS Reduce the amount of granola to 1½ cups. Add 2 cups plain popped popcorn (about ¼ cup unpopped kernels) with the cereal.

RAISIN GRANOLA PEANUT BUTTER TRAIL BARS Reduce the amount of granola to 2 cups and add 1 cup raisins (dark or golden) with the cereal.

MARSHMALLOW CRISPY SQUARES

At the student union at the University of Wisconsin in Madison, the students line up down the block for these homemade treats at lunchtime. My recipe calls for a little more marshmallow than theirs, and if anyone tells the students in Madison, there'll be a long line at my door—and now yours!

---

4 tablespoons unsalted butter plus
    additional for greasing the pan

½ teaspoon salt

One 10-ounce package mini marshmallows

6 cups Rice Krispies cereal

1· Generously butter a 10-inch-square pan and set aside.

2· Melt the butter with the salt in a heavy large saucepan over low heat.

3· Add the marshmallows and stir until they are completely dissolved and the mixture starts to bubble. With the pan still on the heat, add the cereal all at once and stir gently but quickly to coat the cereal.

4· Immediately pour the mixture into the prepared pan and lightly pat it down to reach the edges.

5· Allow the candy to cool and set up at room temperature, about 4 hours. Remove the candy from the pan in one piece and then cut it into 3-inch squares. Wrap each square in wax paper and store them in an airtight container at room temperature for up to 1 week.

VARIATIONS

CHOCOLATE MARSHMALLOW CRISPY SQUARES Increase butter to 6 tablespoons and add ¼ cup cocoa powder to the melted butter before adding the marshmallows.

The following variations work with the base recipe or with the preceding chocolate variation.

ALMOND MARSHMALLOW CRISPY SQUARES Add 1 cup slivered or sliced almonds to the melted marshmallows before adding the cereal.

CHOCOLATE CHIP MARSHMALLOW CRISPY SQUARES Add 1 cup frozen chocolate chips with the cereal. Freezing the chips will keep them from melting into the candy. However, some will still melt, creating a streaky effect.

COCONUT MARSHMALLOW CRISPY SQUARES Add 1 cup shredded, sweetened coconut to the melted marshmallows before adding the cereal.

CRANBERRY MARSHMALLOW CRISPY SQUARES Add 1 cup dried whole cranberries to the melted marshmallows before adding the cereal.

GINGER MARSHMALLOW CRISPY SQUARES Add 1 cup finely chopped candied ginger to the melted marshmallows before adding the cereal.

PIÑA COLADA MARSHMALLOW CRISPY SQUARES Add ½ cup finely chopped dried pineapple and ½ cup shredded sweetened coconut to the melted marshmallows before adding the cereal.

PINEAPPLE MARSHMALLOW CRISPY SQUARES Add 1 cup finely chopped dried pineapple to the melted marshmallows before adding the cereal.

RAISIN MARSHMALLOW CRISPY SQUARES Add 1 cup whole golden raisins to the melted marshmallows before adding the cereal.

MARZIPAN POTATOES

Potatoes are the easiest shapes to make with marzipan. All you need to do is make irregular oblong shapes. A little cocoa powder on the outside simulates dirt. Other shapes like fruits and vegetables can be made with a little more work. Almond paste is available at many supermarkets in the baking aisle. If you can't find it there, check the Source Guide (page 242).

> 7 ounces almond paste
>
> ¼ cup marshmallow cream
>
> 2 tablespoons light corn syrup
>
> 1 cup confectioners' sugar plus more as
>   needed
>
> ¼ cup cocoa powder for coating

1· Combine the almond paste, marshmallow cream, and corn syrup in a large mixing bowl. Beat by hand or with an electric mixer on medium speed, until the ingredients are thoroughly combined. Slowly add the 1 cup confectioners' sugar and mix until a semifirm dough is formed.

2· Turn the dough onto a cutting board or counter and knead the dough for a few minutes to ensure that all the ingredients are well blended and the marzipan is smooth. Add more confectioners' sugar, 1 tablespoon at a time, as necessary until the mixture is firm enough to hold its shape when rolled into a ball, but will still be tender when you bite into it.

3· Roll the marzipan into 1-inch-long oblong balls (about the size of small new potatoes). Keep them irregular in shape to mimic the natural shape of the potato. Roll the balls in the cocoa powder to simulate the dirt found on potatoes and to help keep the balls from drying out. Store the marzipan in layers, separated by wax paper, in an airtight container at room temperature or in the refrigerator for up to 3 weeks.

VARIATIONS

MARZIPAN CHOCOLATES Shape the marzipan into small squares or rectangles and dip them into melted chocolate (milk, white, or semisweet). For advice on melting chocolate, see page 11.

MARZIPAN FRUITS AND VEGETABLES Add a few drops of food coloring with the corn syrup. Shape the marzipan to resemble any fruit or vegetable you desire, including apples, bananas, pears, lemons, oranges, strawberries, carrots, beets, string beans, yams, or tomatoes. For realistic texture and color, use fruit- and vegetable-shaped molds. For texture, you can also roll the shaped fruit or vegetable over a small hand grater to simulate the natural peel or rind. If desired, use a small paintbrush to paint colored details on the shapes. For edible food paints and marzipan fruit and vegetable molds, check the Source Guide on page 242.

RAINBOW MARZIPAN TREATS Divide the dough into four pieces and knead in 4 or 5 drops of different food coloring to each one (I like to use red, yellow, green, and blue). Using a rolling pin, roll each colored piece to ¼ inch thick. Stack the sheets together and press down lightly to help them stick together. Use a sharp knife to cut the marzipan into bite-sized squares or rectangles. Wrap each one in wax paper or dip in melted chocolate (white, milk, or semisweet). For advice on melting chocolate, see page 11.

MINT BARK

Don't know what to do with all those leftover candy canes you used to decorate your house and Christmas tree? Crush them up and mix them into melted white chocolate for a flavor combination that is unbeatable. Six to eight small candy canes or 4 ounces of hard peppermint candies will yield about ⅔ cup crumbled peppermint candy. To crumble hard candy or candy canes, simply place them in a doubled paper or plastic bag and hit them a few times with a heavy pot. Don't overdo it, or you'll have candy powder, not candy crumbs.

> 12 ounces white chocolate, coarsely chopped, or 12 ounces white chocolate chips
>
> ⅔ cup crumbled peppermint candy (see above)
>
> Butter or margarine for greasing the cookie sheet

1· Butter a large cookie sheet and line it with wax paper. Set aside.

2· Melt 6 ounces of the white chocolate in the top of a double boiler set over hot water. If you don't have a double boiler, simply place the chocolate in a bowl that fits snugly over a pot of hot water.

3· When the chocolate has melted completely, remove the top part of the double boiler or the bowl from the hot water. Add the remaining 6 ounces of white chocolate and stir until all of the chocolate is melted and smooth.

4· Insert a candy thermometer or chocolate thermometer into the melted chocolate. Its temperature should be 86 to 88°F. If the chocolate is too cold, place it back over the hot water until the temperature reaches 86 to 88°F. If it is too hot, let it cool until the desired temperature is reached.

5· Add the crumbled candy all at once and mix with a wooden spoon until the chocolate and candy are thoroughly combined.

6. Pour the chocolate mixture onto the prepared cookie sheet, and spread it with a spatula or wooden spoon to about a ½-inch thickness. Don't worry if the chocolate doesn't reach the sides and corners of the cookie sheet; a free-form shape is preferred.

7. Let the bark set up and harden at room temperature, about 4 hours. The cooler your room's temperature, the faster the bark will harden. You can speed up the process by first placing the bark in the refrigerator for 10 minutes, but no longer.

8. Grab the edges of the cooled bark and peel it off the wax paper in one piece, if possible. Break the bark with your hands into irregular pieces, about the size of a credit card. Store the candy in an airtight container at room temperature for up to 1 month.

VARIATIONS

MILK CHOCOLATE MINT BARK Substitute 12 ounces milk chocolate for the white chocolate.

SEMISWEET CHOCOLATE MINT BARK Substitute 12 ounces semisweet chocolate for the white chocolate.

The following variations work with the base recipe or with either of the preceding chocolate variations.

DOUBLE MINT WHITE CHOCOLATE BARK Add ½ teaspoon mint extract with the crumbled candy to the melted chocolate.

HOLIDAY MINT CHOCOLATE BARK Mix 2 or 3 drops of red or green food coloring with the crushed candy into the melted white chocolate.

LEMON MINT BARK Reduce the crumbled peppermint candy to ⅓ cup. Add ⅓ cup crumbled lemon drops with the remaining crumbled peppermint candy.

PARTY MIX

This is a sweet variation of the savory Chex party mix we've all come to love. It's great for holiday parties all year round. I like to keep a large container on hand to serve with drinks.

> 4 cups Life cereal
>
> 2 cups plain popped popcorn (about ¼ cup unpopped kernels)
>
> 1 cup Animal Crackers
>
> 1 cup honey roasted peanuts
>
> 1 cup raisins
>
> 1 cup miniature pretzels
>
> ⅓ cup unsalted butter
>
> ½ cup brown sugar
>
> ¼ cup honey

1· Preheat the oven to 200°F.

2· Combine the cereal, popped popcorn, Animal Crackers, peanuts, raisins, and pretzels in a large bowl. Set aside.

3· Melt the butter in a small saucepan over low heat. Add the brown sugar and honey. Stir until the sugar dissolves completely. Raise the heat to medium and bring the mixture to a boil. Cook for 1 minute. Pour the syrup over the cereal mixture and toss until the mixture is well coated.

4· Spread the mixture onto a jelly-roll pan or into an 11 × 17-inch baking pan and bake for 1 hour, stirring every 15 minutes. Cool the party mix and store it in an airtight container at room temperature for up to 1 month.

VARIATION

SPICY PARTY MIX Increase the butter to ½ cup and omit the brown sugar. Add 2 teaspoons Tabasco sauce, 1 tablespoon Worcestershire sauce, 1 teaspoon onion powder, 1 teaspoon garlic powder, and 1 tablespoon ground chili powder to the melted butter.

PEANUT CLUSTERS

Salted peanuts and dark chocolate—two ingredients, many happy friends.

> 16 ounces semisweet chocolate, coarsely chopped, or 16 ounces semisweet chocolate chips
>
> ¾ cup salted, roasted peanuts
>
> Butter or margarine for greasing the cookie sheet

1· Grease a large cookie sheet and line it with wax paper. Set aside.

2· Melt 8 ounces of the semisweet chocolate in the top of a double boiler set over hot water. If you don't have a double boiler, simply place the chocolate in a bowl that fits snugly over a pot of hot water.

3· When the chocolate has melted completely, remove the top part of the double boiler or the bowl from the hot water. Add the remaining 8 ounces of semisweet chocolate and stir until all of the chocolate is melted and smooth.

4· Insert a candy thermometer or chocolate thermometer into the melted chocolate. Its temperature should be 88 to 90°F. If the chocolate is too cold, place it back over the hot water until the temperature reaches 88 to 90°F. If it is too hot, let it cool until the desired temperature is reached.

5· Add the peanuts all at once and stir with a wooden spoon until the nuts are completely coated with chocolate.

6· Drop by tablespoonful onto the prepared cookie sheet. Let the clusters harden at room temperature, about 4 hours. The cooler your room's temperature, the faster the chocolate will harden. You can speed up the process by first placing the clusters in the refrigerator for 10 minutes, but no longer.

7· Store the clusters in an airtight container at room temperature for up to 1 month.

VARIATIONS

MILK CHOCOLATE PEANUT CLUSTERS Substitute 16 ounces milk chocolate chips for the semisweet chips.

WHITE CHOCOLATE PEANUT CLUSTERS Substitute 16 ounces white chocolate chips for the semisweet chips.

The following variations work with the base recipe or with either of the preceding chocolate variations.

ALMOND CLUSTERS Substitute ¾ cup toasted slivered almonds for the peanuts. For information on toasting nuts, see page 12.

CASHEW CLUSTERS Substitute ¾ cup toasted halved cashews for the peanuts. For information on toasting nuts, see page 12.

CINNAMON PEANUT CLUSTERS Add ½ teaspoon ground cinnamon with the peanuts to the melted chocolate.

PEANUT RAISIN CLUSTERS Reduce the peanuts to ½ cup. Add ¼ cup raisins (dark or golden) with the remaining peanuts to the chocolate.

POPCORN BALLS

Some classics can't be improved. But they can be made easier. Melted marshmallows hold these popcorn balls together and make them a snap to prepare. Even making your own popcorn is easy if you use Jiffy Pop or your microwave.

¼ cup unsalted butter plus additional for greasing the cookie sheet (and your fingertips)

16 ounces miniature marshmallows

½ teaspoon salt

12 cups homemade popped popcorn (about 1½ cups unpopped kernels)

1· Butter a large cookie sheet and line it with wax paper. Set aside.

2· Melt the ¼ cup butter in a heavy large saucepan over low heat. Add the marshmallows and salt. Stir until the marshmallows have completely melted and the mixture starts to bubble. Add the popcorn all at once and stir gently to coat each piece. Remove the mixture from the heat and let it cool, about 5 minutes.

3· With lightly buttered fingers, pinch off small handfuls of the popcorn mixture (about the size of a tangerine) and roll them into balls. Rebutter your hands as often as necessary to prevent sticking.

4· Place the popcorn balls on the prepared cookie sheet and allow them to cool completely, about 1 hour. Store the popcorn balls in an airtight container at room temperature for up to 2 weeks.

VARIATIONS

CANDY POPCORN BALLS Reduce the amount of popcorn by 2 cups. Add 2 cups small candies such as M&M's, chocolate-covered raisins, chocolate-covered peanuts, or candy hearts with the popcorn.

CASHEW RAISIN POPCORN BALLS Reduce the amount of popcorn by 2 cups. Add 1 cup roasted cashews and 1 cup raisins with the popcorn.

CHOCOLATE PEANUT POPCORN BALLS Reduce the amount of popcorn by 2 cups. Add 1 cup roasted peanuts and 1 cup semisweet chocolate chips with the popcorn.

DOUBLE MARSHMALLOW POPCORN BALLS Shape each ball around a large marshmallow as its center.

PISTACHIO CHERRY POPCORN BALLS Add 1 cup shelled pistachios and 1 cup finely chopped dried cherries with the popcorn.

SESAME CRUNCH POPCORN BALLS Reduce the amount of popcorn by 1 cup. Add 2 cups finely chopped Sesame Crunch (page 235) with the popcorn.

RAISIN CLUSTERS

What's better than a handful of Raisinets? A handful of raisin clusters made from rich dark chocolate and plump juicy raisins. Take these to the movies with you if you can sneak them past the guard.

> 16 ounces semisweet chocolate, coarsely chopped, or 16 ounces semisweet chocolate chips
>
> ¾ cup raisins (dark or golden)
>
> Butter or margarine for greasing the cookie sheet

1· Butter a large cookie sheet and line it with wax paper. Set aside.

2· Melt 8 ounces of the semisweet chocolate in the top of a double boiler set over hot water. If you don't have a double boiler, simply place the chocolate in a bowl that fits snugly over a pot of hot water.

3· When the chocolate has melted completely, remove the top part of the double boiler or the bowl from the hot water. Add the remaining 8 ounces of semisweet chocolate and stir until all of the chocolate is melted and smooth.

4· Insert a candy thermometer or chocolate thermometer into the melted chocolate. Its temperature should be 88 to 90°F. If the chocolate is too cold, place it back over the hot water until the temperature reaches 88 to 90°F. If it is too hot, let it cool until the desired temperature is reached.

5· Add the raisins all at once and stir with a wooden spoon until the raisins are completely coated with chocolate.

6· Drop by tablespoonsful onto the prepared cookie sheet. Let the clusters harden at room temperature, about 4 hours. The cooler your room's temperature, the faster the chocolate will harden. You can speed up the process by first placing the clusters in the refrigerator for 10 minutes, but no longer.

7· Store the clusters in an airtight container at room temperature for up to 1 month.

VARIATIONS

MILK CHOCOLATE RAISIN CLUSTERS Substitute 16 ounces milk chocolate chips for the semisweet chips.

WHITE CHOCOLATE RAISIN CLUSTERS Substitute 16 ounces white chocolate chips for the semisweet chips.

The following variations work with the base recipe or with either of the preceding chocolate variations.

APRICOT CLUSTERS Substitute ¾ cup roughly chopped dried apricots for the raisins.

BLUEBERRY CLUSTERS Substitute ¾ cup whole dried blueberries for the raisins.

CHERRY CLUSTERS Substitute ¾ cup whole dried cherries for the raisins.

CRANBERRY CLUSTERS Substitute ¾ cup whole dried cranberries for the raisins.

DATE CLUSTERS Substitute ¾ cup roughly chopped dried dates for the raisins.

FIG CLUSTERS Substitute ¾ cup roughly chopped dried figs for the raisins.

ROCKY ROAD DROPS

This recipe combines the ease of no-fail fudge with the classic combination of chocolate, marshmallows, and almonds.

> Butter or margarine for greasing the cookie sheet
>
> 12 ounces semisweet chocolate, coarsely chopped, or 12 ounces semisweet chocolate chips
>
> 2 cups miniature marshmallows
>
> 1 cup slivered almonds, toasted (see page 12)

1· Butter a large cookie sheet and line it with wax paper. Set aside.

2· Melt 6 ounces of the semisweet chocolate in the top of a double boiler set over hot water. If you don't have a double boiler, simply place the chocolate in a bowl that fits snugly over a pot of hot water.

3· When the chocolate has melted completely, remove the top part of the double boiler or the bowl from the hot water. Add the remaining 6 ounces of semisweet chocolate and stir until all of the chocolate is melted and smooth.

4· Insert a candy thermometer or chocolate thermometer into the melted chocolate. Its temperature should be 88 to 90°F. If the chocolate is too cold, place it back over the hot water until the temperature reaches 88 to 90°F. If it is too hot, let it cool until the desired temperature is reached.

5· Add the marshmallows and nuts all at once and stir with a wooden spoon until the nuts and marshmallows are completely coated with chocolate.

6· Drop by tablespoonsful onto the prepared cookie sheet. Place in the refrigerator until the drops are firm, about 1 hour. Store the drops in an airtight container in the refrigerator for up to 1 month.

CRUNCHY CHEWY ROCKY ROAD DROPS Reduce the amount of the marshmallows by 1 cup. Add 1 cup Cracker Jack candy with the nuts to the chocolate.

ROCKY ROAD SQUARES Increase the marshmallows to 4 cups. Pour the finished mixture into a greased 9-inch baking pan lined with wax paper. Do not flatten, since the top should resemble a rocky road. Set in refrigerator to chill. Cut into 2-inch squares when firm.

SALTY PEANUT ROCKY ROAD Substitute 1 cup salted peanuts for the almonds.

SOUTHWEST ROCKY ROAD DROPS Add 1 tablespoon ancho chili powder to the melted chocolate before adding the marshmallows and nuts. Substitute 1 cup pecans for the almonds.

WASHINGTON STATE ROCKY ROAD DROPS Reduce the amount of marshmallows by 1 cup. Add ½ cup whole dried cherries with the nuts to the chocolate.

ROLLED MARSHMALLOW POPS

Your kids will think these brightly colored candies are magic wands—glittering pink marsh-mallows atop lollipop sticks. Colored sugar and lollipop sticks are available at many specialty stores. Or consult the Source Guide on page 242.

> 1 cup pink-colored sugar
> 24 regular marshmallows
> 24 lollipop sticks

1· Place the sugar on a small plate and set it aside.

2· Bring a small pan of water to a simmer over medium heat.

3· Insert one stick into each marshmallow. Hold one marshmallow over the simmering water, turning it around until the steam softens the outside and makes it sticky. Immediately roll the marshmallow in the pink sugar, making sure to cover the top and bottom. Place the pop, stick up, onto a large platter. Repeat with the remaining marshmallows.

4· When the pops are dry, about 1 hour, store them in layers, separated by wax paper, in an airtight container at room temperature for up to 1 month.

VARIATIONS

CINNAMON SUGAR MARSHMALLOW POPS Substitute cinnamon sugar for the colored sugar. To make cinnamon sugar, mix together 1 tablespoon ground cinnamon with 1 cup granulated sugar until well blended.

COCOA MARSHMALLOW POPS Substitute 1 cup sifted cocoa powder for the colored sugar.

HALLOWEEN MARSHMALLOW POPS Substitute 1 cup orange and black sprinkles for the pink sugar.

NUTTY MARSHMALLOW POPS Substitute 1 cup finely chopped peanuts for the colored sugar.

RAINBOW MARSHMALLOW POPS Use any combination of red, green, blue, orange, red, yellow, and pink sugar, placing each color on a different plate. Dip the tops of the steamed marshmallows in one color, and make the sides and bottoms as many colors as you like.

TOASTED COCONUT MARSHMALLOW POPS Substitute 1 cup toasted, shredded sweetened coconut for the colored sugar. (For advice on toasting coconut, see page 12).

SUGARPLUMS

The children were tucked away safe in their beds
While visions of sugarplums danced in their heads.

—CLEMENT CLARKE MOORE

MAKES ABOUT 2 DOZEN SUGARPLUMS

Everyone knows the poem but very few could tell you what sugarplums actually are. They are simply dried plums pureed with brandy, shaped into balls, and rolled in sugar.

> 1 cup chopped pitted prunes
> 1 cup golden raisins
> ⅓ cup slivered almonds
> 2 tablespoons brandy or Armagnac
> ¼ cup superfine sugar, for coating

1· Place the prunes, raisins, almonds, and brandy in a food processor. Pulse on and off 10 times or until the mixture forms a thick paste.

2· Wet your hands and roll heaping teaspoonsful of the fruit mixture into balls between your palms. Roll each ball in superfine sugar. Store the candies in an airtight container at room temperature for up to 2 weeks.

3· Sugarplums are best made 12 to 24 hours in advance. If desired, reroll the sugarplums in superfine sugar just before serving.

VARIATIONS

APPLE ORCHARD SUGARPLUMS Substitute 1 cup chopped dried apples for the raisins and 2 tablespoons Calvados for the brandy.

CHERRY TREE SUGARPLUMS Reduce the amount of raisins to ½ cup. Add ½ cup whole dried cherries with the remaining raisins. Substitute 2 tablespoons kirsch for the brandy.

CRANBERRY SUGARPLUMS Substitute 1 cup dried cranberries for the raisins and 2 tablespoons vodka for the brandy.

PEAR SUGARPLUMS Substitute 1 cup roughly chopped dried pears for the raisins and 2 tablespoons white rum for the brandy.

PINEAPPLE SUGARPLUMS Substitute 1 cup roughly chopped dried pineapple for the raisins and 2 tablespoons golden rum for the brandy.

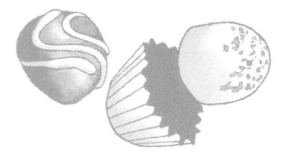

TRAIL MIX

Any of these three variations is perfect for a long hike in the woods, a car ride to grandma's, or that three-hour movie you keep meaning to rent.

Combine all the ingredients called for in a large bowl and toss well. Store the trail mix in an airtight container at room temperature for up to 1 month.

CHOCOLATE TRAIL MIX

¾ cup chocolate-covered raisins

¾ cup chocolate-covered peanuts

¾ cup chocolate-covered almonds

¾ cup M&M's candies

¾ cup chocolate-covered pretzels

½ cup white chocolate chips

FRUIT AND NUT TRAIL MIX

¾ cup raisins

¾ cup dried cranberries

¾ cup chopped dried apricots

¾ cup salted peanuts

¾ cup toasted almonds

½ cup shelled sunflower seeds

TROPICAL TRAIL MIX

¾ cup chopped dried pineapple

¾ cup chopped dried papaya

¾ cup banana chips

¾ cup macadamia nuts

¾ cup toasted cashews

½ cup shredded sweetened coconut

TROPICAL CLUSTERS

Close your eyes and imagine you're on a Caribbean island. The scents of bananas, papayas, and coconut fill the air. The only thing that can improve this fantasy is mixing these flavors with rich, creamy white chocolate. Paradise found!

> 16 ounces white chocolate, coarsely chopped, or 16 ounces white chocolate chips
>
> ¼ cup chopped dried papaya
>
> ¼ cup chopped dried banana
>
> ¼ cup unsweetened coconut chips
>
> Butter or margarine for greasing the cookie sheet

1· Butter a large cookie sheet and line it with wax paper. Set aside.

2· Melt 8 ounces of the white chocolate in the top of a double boiler set over hot water. If you don't have a double boiler, simply place the chocolate in a bowl that fits snugly over a pot of hot water.

3· When the chocolate has melted completely, remove the top part of the double boiler or the bowl from the hot water. Add the remaining 8 ounces of white chocolate and stir until all of the chocolate is melted and smooth.

4· Insert a candy thermometer or chocolate thermometer into the melted chocolate. Its temperature should be 86 to 88°F. If the chocolate is too cold, place it back over the hot water until the temperature reaches 86 to 88°F. If it is too hot, let it cool until the desired temperature is reached.

5· Add the dried papaya, dried banana, and coconut chips all at once and stir with a wooden spoon until the fruit is completely coated with chocolate.

6· Drop by tablespoonful onto the prepared cookie sheet. The clusters will firm up at room temperature in about 4 hours, or you can place them in the refrigerator for 1 hour. Store the clusters in an airtight container in the refrigerator or at room temperature for up to 1 month.

VARIATIONS

HAWAIIAN CLUSTERS Substitute ¼ cup chopped macadamia nuts for the chopped papaya.

MEDITERRANEAN CLUSTERS Instead of the papaya, banana, and coconut, substitute ½ cup each of coarsely chopped dried figs, coarsely chopped dried dates, and toasted chickpeas. Do not use canned chickpeas. Toasted chickpeas are a dry snack available at gourmet stores, or consult the Source Guide on page 242.

MEXICAN TROPICAL CLUSTERS Add 1 teaspoon ground cinnamon and 1 teaspoon crushed red chili flakes to the melted chocolate with the dried fruit.

TROPICAL COCKTAIL CLUSTERS Add 1 teaspoon artificial rum flavoring to the melted chocolate with the dried fruit.

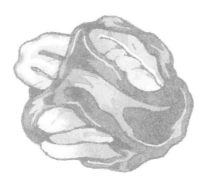

S O F T *and* C H E W Y
T r e a t s

WHEN YOU THINK OF INDULGENT candy, the first things that might come to mind are truffles, chocolate creams, chocolate-covered cherries, nougat, caramels, and pralines. These are the pinnacle of candy making—fancy and not so fancy treats that fill the shelves of candy stores and fudge shops all over the world. No matter where we travel, my best friend says that the real money is in fudge. Given the number of stores I've found, I think he's right. I've put together as many recipes as I could for you to make at home that rival the best I've had from these candy emporiums. Make the treats for your family and friends, and they'll think you've been to chef school. But keep some for yourself, just because you deserve it!

APPLE CANDY

Although an apple a day is said to keep the doctor away, one piece of apple candy a day probably won't keep the dentist away. Well, at least these chewy little squares are fat-free!

> 2 envelopes unflavored gelatin
>
> ½ cup cold water
>
> 1 tablespoon cornstarch
>
> 1 tablespoon lemon juice
>
> 2 cups unsweetened applesauce (jarred or homemade)
>
> 1 cup granulated sugar
>
> 1 cup light brown sugar
>
> ¼ teaspoon salt
>
> 1 cup confectioners' sugar, for coating

1· Sprinkle the gelatin over the cold water in a small bowl and set aside to soften, about 5 minutes.

2· Dissolve the cornstarch in the lemon juice and set aside.

3· Place the applesauce in a heavy medium pan and set it over medium heat. Add the granulated sugar, brown sugar, and salt. Stir until the sugars dissolve completely and the mixture comes to a simmer. Continue to cook, stirring often, for 5 minutes.

4· Reduce the heat to low and add the softened gelatin. Stir until the gelatin is completely dissolved. Add the cornstarch and lemon juice mixture. Cook for 2 minutes or until the mixture thickens. Remove the pan from the heat.

5· Rinse an 8-inch or 9-inch square pan (preferably nonstick) with cold water but do not dry it. Using a wet spatula, spread the mixture into the pan. Allow it to sit at room temperature overnight.

6· Sift ¼ cup confectioners' sugar over the top of the candy. Dust your counter or a large cutting board with ¼ cup additional confectioners' sugar. Turn the pan over and remove the candy from the pan in one piece, using your fingers to help peel it out of the pan. Place the candy sugared side down onto the prepared work surface. Using a small sharp knife, cut the candy into 1-inch squares and use the remaining ½ cup confectioners' sugar to coat the candies to keep them from sticking together.

7· Store the candy in layers, separated by wax paper, in an airtight container at room temperature or in the refrigerator for up to 2 weeks.

VARIATIONS

APPLE ALMOND CANDY Add ½ teaspoon almond extract to the pan with the cornstarch and lemon juice mixture. If desired, add ¾ cup sliced almond with the almond extract.

APPLE CRANBERRY CANDY Reduce the amount of applesauce to 1 cup. Add 1 cup cranberry sauce with the remaining applesauce.

APPLE PIE CANDY Add ½ teaspoon ground cinnamon, ¼ teaspoon ground cloves, ⅛ teaspoon ground nutmeg, and ⅛ teaspoon ground mace to the pan with the applesauce. Alternatively, use 1 teaspoon apple pie spice mix.

APPLE WALNUT CANDY Add ¾ cup chopped walnuts with the cornstarch and lemon juice mixture.

PEAR CANDY Substitute pear sauce for the applesauce. To make pear sauce, puree 4 large, canned, drained pears in a blender or food processor. You should have about 2½ cups of puree. If not, add another pear. Then cook the pear puree over medium heat in a heavy pan, stirring constantly. It's ready when it has reduced to 2 cups and has thickened slightly.

BURNT SUGAR FUDGE

This fudge is not a chocolate confection. It has a fudgy texture, but gets its distinctive flavor from the caramelized sugar—an unexpected yet delicious variation. Be careful caramelizing the sugar. It is very hot and can cause severe burns.

> 2 cups sugar
>
> ⅔ cup cream
>
> 1 tablespoon butter plus additional for greasing the pan
>
> 1 teaspoon vanilla extract

1· Line a 10-inch square pan with wax paper, overlapping the edges at least 2 inches. Butter the paper and set the pan aside.

2· Place ¾ cup sugar in a tall-sided heavy saucepan. Height is important because adding the cream later will cause the syrup to boil high in the pan, and you don't want the syrup to boil over.

3· Place the pan over medium heat and stir constantly with a large wooden spoon until the sugar melts and turns amber.

4· Stirring constantly, add the remaining sugar and the cream to the pan. The mixture will instantly boil high in the pan. Continue stirring to keep it from boiling over. The already "burnt" sugar may also seize into a hard lump on the bottom of the pan. Continue stirring until the sugar dissolves and the mixture is homogenous.

5· Clip a candy thermometer to the inside of the pan. Bring the mixture to a boil and cook, without stirring, until it reaches 240°F (soft ball).

6· Remove the pan from the heat and allow the mixture to cool undisturbed until the thermometer reads 110°F.

7· Add the butter and vanilla all at once. Stir vigorously with a wooden spoon until the mixture loses its gloss and thickens to the consistency of cake icing. Using a buttered spatula, spread the mixture into the prepared pan and place it in the refrigerator to cool for at least 8 hours.

8· Grab the edges of the wax paper and pull the candy out of the pan. Using a sharp knife, cut the fudge into bite-sized pieces. Store them in layers, separated by wax paper, in an airtight container in the refrigerator for up to 1 week.

VARIATIONS

BURNT SUGAR APRICOT FUDGE After the fudge cools to 110°F, stir in ½ cup finely chopped dried apricots.

BURNT SUGAR MEXICAN FUDGE Add ½ teaspoon ground cinnamon with the cream. After the fudge cools to 110°F, stir in ½ cup sliced almonds.

BURNT SUGAR NUT FUDGE After the fudge cools to 110°F, stir in ½ cup nuts such as pecan pieces, walnut pieces, slivered almonds, or chopped cashews.

BURNT SUGAR RUM RAISIN FUDGE After the fudge cools to 110°F, stir in ½ cup golden raisins. Also substitute 1 teaspoon rum extract for the vanilla extract.

BUTTERCREAM TRUFFLES

Truffles are perhaps the most elegant of all candies. They resemble the expensive fungus they're named for, but they have nothing else in common. This recipe uses a basic butter-cream which combines butter with powdered sugar for its base. These truffles are best eaten at room temperature, but need to be kept refrigerated.

> 6 ounces unsweetened chocolate
> ⅔ cup unsalted butter, at room temperature
> 2⅓ cups confectioners' sugar
> ⅓ cup heavy cream
> 1 tablespoon vanilla extract
> Cocoa powder for coating

1· Melt the unsweetened chocolate in the top part of a double boiler set over hot water, or in a bowl that fits snugly over a pot of hot water. Set the melted chocolate aside.

2· Combine the butter and confectioners' sugar in a large bowl. Beat with an electric mixer on medium speed until the mixture is smooth and pale yellow. Turn the mixer to low and beat in the heavy cream. Quickly add the melted chocolate and vanilla, beating just long enough to make a smooth paste without any chocolate streaks.

3· Refrigerate the mixture until it is cool and firm, 1 to 2 hours.

4· Scoop out heaping teaspoonsful of the chocolate mixture and quickly roll each one into a ball between your palms. If the chocolate gets too warm, it will melt in your hands. If this happens, refrigerate the mixture again until it's easier to handle. Alternately, use a ½-ounce ice cream scoop to make perfectly round truffles that don't need to be rolled in your hands.

5· Roll the truffles in cocoa powder. Shake off any excess cocoa and store the truffles in layers, separated by wax paper, in an airtight container in the refrigerator for up to 2 weeks. Allow the truffles to come to room temperature before serving.

ALMOND BUTTERCREAM TRUFFLES Substitute 1 teaspoon almond extract for the vanilla extract.

BANANA BUTTERCREAM TRUFFLES Reduce the amount of vanilla extract to 1 teaspoon. Add 2 teaspoons banana flavoring with the remaining vanilla.

MOCHA BUTTERCREAM TRUFFLES Mix 1 tablespoon instant espresso into the vanilla extract. Be sure that the espresso is completely dissolved before adding it to the chocolate mixture.

ORANGE BUTTERCREAM TRUFFLES Add 1 tablespoon melted orange juice concentrate with the vanilla.

RUM BUTTERCREAM TRUFFLES Substitute 1 tablespoon artificial rum flavoring for the vanilla extract.

BUTTERMILK PRALINES

People in Dallas often send huge baskets of buttermilk pralines from Neiman Marcus as Christmas presents. Now these creamy pecan candies can come from your kitchen any time of the year. Place them in a small wicker basket lined with colored tissue paper for a traditional Southern gift.

3 cups sugar

1 cup buttermilk

1 cup unsalted butter, at room temperature, plus additional for greasing the cookie sheets

2 tablespoons light corn syrup

1 teaspoon baking soda

¼ teaspoon salt

2 teaspoons vanilla extract

2½ cups pecan halves

1· Butter 2 large cookie sheets and line them with wax paper. Set aside.

2· Combine the sugar, buttermilk, 1 cup butter, corn syrup, baking soda, and salt in a heavy, tall-sided saucepan. Height is important because the buttermilk will cause the sugar syrup to boil high in the pan. You don't want this spilling over.

3· Place the pan over low heat and stir until the sugar completely dissolves and the mixture comes to a simmer.

4· Clip a candy thermometer to the inside of the pan. Raise the heat to medium and bring the mixture to a boil without stirring. Continue to cook, stirring occasionally, until the mixture reaches 260°F (hard ball).

5· Remove the pan from the heat and add the vanilla and pecans. Stir just until the pecans are coated. Too much stirring can cause the candy to crystallize and become grainy—though still quite delicious.

6· Drop tablespoonsful of the hot candy onto the prepared cookie sheets, leaving a few inches between each to allow for spreading. Let the candy sit at room temperature until it is cool and has firmed up, 2 to 3 hours.

7· Peel the candies off the paper and store them in an airtight container at room temperature for up to 2 weeks.

VARIATIONS

RUM PRALINES Add 2 teaspoons artificial rum flavoring with the vanilla.

TABASCO PRALINES Add 1 teaspoon Tabasco sauce (or more if desired) with the sugar.

CARAMELS

Although you can form these caramels in almost any pan, soft, flexible candy molds make it easier. It's not as extravagant as it sounds—after all, you wouldn't make muffins without a muffin tin. Besides, candy molds are not expensive, and your caramels will be a uniform shape and size, making them easier to wrap and store. I prefer simple square or rectangular molds, but you can choose anything from heart shapes to alligators. See the Source Guide on page 242.

> 1 cup heavy cream
>
> 1 cup sugar
>
> 1 cup light corn syrup
>
> ¼ teaspoon salt
>
> 4 tablespoons unsalted butter plus
>   additional for greasing the pan or molds

1· Butter a 10-inch square pan or flexible hard candy molds. Set aside.

2· Combine the cream, sugar, corn syrup, and salt in a tall-sided heavy saucepan. Height is important because the cream will cause the sugar syrup to boil up high in the pan. It can cause quite a mess if it spills over.

3· Place the pan over medium heat and stir until the sugar is completely dissolved. Add the butter and stir until it melts into the sugar syrup.

4· Clip a candy thermometer to the inside of the pan. Cook the mixture, without stirring, until the temperature reaches 248°F (firm ball).

5· Pour the hot caramel into the prepared pan and set it aside to cool slightly. When the caramel candy is cool enough to handle but still warm to the touch, use a flexible spatula to remove the caramel from the pan in one piece. Place the caramel on a cutting board and use a sharp knife to cut the candy into 1-inch squares. If you wait until the caramel is cold, it will be difficult to cut.

6· If you're using candy molds, first pour the hot caramel into a Pyrex measuring cup with a handle and spout. This will make it easier to pour the caramel into the small molds. Slowly fill the molds just to the top. Let the caramels cool completely before popping them out of the molds, about 2 hours.

7· Wrap each caramel in wax paper and store them all in an airtight container at room temperature for up to 3 weeks.

VARIATIONS

ALMOND CARAMEL Stir in ½ teaspoon almond extract and ½ cup sliced almonds (optional) before pouring the caramel into the pan or the molds.

COCONUT CARAMEL Reduce the amount of cream to ½ cup. Add ½ cup unsweetened coconut milk with the remaining cream.

COFFEE CARAMEL Warm the cream and add 1 tablespoon instant espresso powder to it. Stir until it completely dissolves, then add the coffee-flavored cream with the sugar and the corn syrup.

RUM CARAMEL Stir in 1 tablespoon rum extract before pouring the hot caramel into the pan or the molds.

VANILLA CARAMEL Stir in 1 tablespoon vanilla extract before pouring the hot caramel into the pan or the molds.

CARAMEL APPLES

MAKES 10 TO 12 APPLES

Macouns. Granny Smiths. Red Delicious. Jonagolds. McIntoshes—all are perfect for caramel apples. Red or green, as long as they are crisp!

> 10 to 12 medium apples
> 10 to 12 tall wooden lollipop sticks or chopsticks
> 3 cups sugar
> ¾ cup light corn syrup
> 2 cups evaporated milk
> 2 tablespoons butter plus additional for greasing the cookie sheet

1· Butter a large cookie sheet and line it with parchment paper. Butter the paper and set the sheet aside.

2· Wash and thoroughly dry the apples. Remove the stems and turn the apples upside down. Since the tops are usually larger and flatter, the apples should stay upright. Insert a wooden stick into the base of each apple, pushing about two-thirds of the way through. Set the prepared apples aside.

3· Combine the sugar, corn syrup, and ½ cup evaporated milk in a heavy large saucepan. Place over medium heat and stir until the sugar dissolves and the mixture comes to a boil. Allow the mixture to boil without stirring until it thickens and turns golden.

4· Remove the pan from the heat and slowly stir in the remaining 1½ cups evaporated milk and the 2 tablespoons butter. Stir constantly as the mixture will rise up and foam.

5· When the foaming subsides, clip a candy thermometer to the inside of the pan. Continue cooking the caramel, stirring constantly, until it reaches 240°F (soft ball). Remove the pan from the heat and set it aside until the caramel stops bubbling.

6· Tilt the pan to create a deep pool of caramel. Dip one apple into the caramel, turning it as necessary to coat it completely. Allow any excess caramel to drip back into the pan, then place the apple on the prepared cookie sheet, stick up. Repeat with the remaining apples. Allow the coated apples to cool before serving, about 2 hours.

7. Loosely wrap the caramel apples in lightly buttered wax paper and store them in a cool place for up to 3 days. Do not refrigerate the dipped apples or the caramel will become too hard to eat.

VARIATIONS

CHOCOLATE CHIP COCONUT CARAMEL APPLES Before making the caramel, fill a small baking pan with equal amounts of shredded sweetened coconut and chocolate chips. You may use milk, semisweet, or white chocolate or any combination as long as you keep the chips and coconut to a depth of ½ inch. Set aside. After dipping one apple in the caramel, allow the excess to drip back into the pan, then immediately stand the apple up on the chip mixture. The chips and coconut will stick to the caramel and create a flat bottom. Roll the apple in the mixture, making sure that the caramel is completely covered with chips and coconut. Place the apple on the prepared cookie sheet and allow it to cool. Repeat with the remaining apples. *Note:* Continue to add more chips and coconut to the pan as needed.

PECAN CARAMEL APPLES Before making the caramel, fill a small baking pan with chopped pecans, at least ½-inch deep. After dipping one apple in the caramel, allow the excess to drip back into the pan, then immediately stand the apple up on the nuts. The nuts will stick to the caramel and create a flat bottom. Roll the apple in the mixture, making sure that the caramel is completely covered with nuts. Place the apple on the prepared cookie sheet and allow it to cool. Repeat with the remaining apples. *Note:* Continue to add more nuts to the pan as needed.

SWEET AND SALTY PEANUT CARAMEL APPLES Before making the caramel, fill a small baking pan with chopped salted peanuts, at least ½-inch deep. After dipping one apple in the caramel, allow the excess to drip back into the pan, then immediately stand the apple up on the nuts. The nuts will stick to the caramel and create a flat bottom. Roll the apple in the mixture, making sure that the caramel is completely covered with nuts. Place the apple on the prepared cookie sheet and allow it to cool. Repeat with the remaining apples. *Note:* Continue to add more nuts to the pan as needed.

TOASTED COCONUT CARAMEL APPLES Before making the caramel, heat the oven to 350°F and spread three 8-ounce packages of sweetened shredded coconut on a baking sheet. Place the coconut in the oven for 10 minutes or until the coconut is lightly toasted. You will need to stir the coconut occasionally to help it brown evenly. Remove the baking sheet from the oven and allow the coconut to cool. Place the cooled toasted coconut in a small clean baking pan to a depth of at least ½ inch. After dipping one apple in the caramel, allow the excess to drip back into the pan, then immediately stand the apple up on the coconut. The coconut will stick to the caramel and create a flat bottom. Roll the apple in the mixture, making sure that the caramel is completely covered with coconut. Place the apple on the prepared cookie sheet and allow it to cool. Repeat with the remaining apples. *Note:* Continue to add more toasted coconut to the pan as needed.

CHEWING GUM

You're thinking, *Wow, I can't wait to try this.* Or, *Why would anyone make their own gum?* Because it's fun, it's messy, and you'll probably be the only one on your block . . . no, in your city who'll ever do it. Homemade gum requires purchased gum base (see the Source Guide on page 242). You'll also need disposable aluminum baking pans and heavy-duty plastic spoons or a couple of strong chopsticks that you don't mind throwing away when you're done.

½ to 1 cup confectioners' sugar

2 ounces gum base

3 tablespoons corn syrup

1 teaspoon peppermint extract *or* ¼ teaspoon peppermint oil

4 to 5 drops green food coloring, optional

1· Place ½ cup confectioners' sugar on the counter. Form it into a small mound and create a well in the center. You will mix the gum base into this later.

2· Meanwhile, place the gum base in an 8-inch round, disposable cake pan. Float this pan in a larger saucepan of water, placed over medium heat. Bring the water to a simmer. Cover the saucepan, reduce the heat, and simmer until the gum base melts, 10 to 15 minutes.

3· While the gum base melts, heat the corn syrup in a small pan over low heat until it is hot but not boiling. Alternatively, heat the corn syrup in a small bowl in the microwave, set on medium, for 30 seconds. Stir the peppermint extract and the food coloring into the hot corn syrup.

4· Remove the small pan containing the melted gum base from the simmering water. Stir in the flavored corn syrup with a heavy disposable plastic spoon or a chopstick. The mixture will be very sticky. Scrape as much of the gum base as possible out of the disposable pan and into the well in the middle of the confectioners' sugar.

5· Using your fingers, work the confectioners' sugar into the gum base until a soft dough is formed. Knead the dough with the heels of your hands, pressing down toward the counter. Add more confectioners' sugar as necessary until the dough is semifirm and no longer sticky.

6· Break off bite-sized pieces of gum and roll into them into balls between your palms. Roll these gum balls into additional confectioners' sugar. Wrap each gum ball in wax paper and store them all in an airtight container at room temperature for up to 2 weeks.

7· Alternatively, the gum can be rolled into thin flat sheets with either a rolling pin or a hand-cranked pasta roller. Cut the thin sheets of gum into sticks using a sharp knife or pizza cutter. Coat each piece with additional confectioners' sugar before wrapping and storing.

8· A dough scraper will usually be enough to remove any gum base that sticks to your counter, but stubborn spots can be dissolved with a little cooking oil.

VARIATIONS

BUBBLE GUM Substitute artificial bubble gum flavoring (see Source Guide, page 242) for the peppermint extract, and red food coloring for the green food coloring. This gum will taste like bubble gum, but you can't blow bubbles with it. Special bubble gum base is needed, and is not readily available to the public.

CANDY-COATED GUM BALLS Use a fork to dip the gum balls into the same syrup used for making Apricot Jewels (page 194). Freeze the gum balls before dipping them, so they won't melt into the hot syrup. Place the dipped gum on oiled parchment paper to cool and harden. Wrap each gum ball in wax paper or store them all in one airtight container. The candy coating may get sticky after a day or two, so share the gum with your friends while it's fresh.

OTHER FLAVORS Any candy natural or artificial flavoring can be used instead of mint. Flavors like clove, cinnamon, tutti-frutti, banana, watermelon, grape, and apple are available by mail (see the Source Guide on page 242). Use 1 teaspoon flavoring per batch. Remember to use the appropriate food coloring to match the flavor you choose.

CHOCOLATE CARAMELS

These have just a hint of chocolate flavor so that the taste of caramel isn't overpowered. The candy can be made in one pan and cut into bite-sized pieces, or use 1¼-inch hard-candy molds.

> 1½ cups light cream
>
> 1¼ cups sugar
>
> 5 tablespoons unsalted butter plus
>   additional for greasing the pan or molds
>
> ½ cup light corn syrup
>
> 2 ounces unsweetened chocolate, coarsely
>   chopped

1· Butter an 8-inch square pan or flexible hard-candy molds (consult the Source Guide on page 242). Set aside.

2· Combine the cream, sugar, 5 tablespoons butter, and corn syrup in a heavy, tall-sided pan. Height is important because the cream will make the syrup boil up high in the pan. It can cause quite a mess if it boils over.

3· Place the pan over medium heat and stir until the sugar dissolves. Add the chocolate and stir until the chocolate melts.

4· Clip a candy thermometer to the inside of the pan. Raise the heat to medium-high and bring the mixture to a boil without stirring. Cook, stirring occasionally, until the mixture reaches 240°F (soft ball).

5· Continue to cook, stirring constantly and vigorously, until the temperature reaches 248°F (firm ball).

6· Pour the hot caramel into the prepared pan and set it aside to cool slightly. When the caramel candy is cool enough to handle but still warm to the touch, use a flexible spatula to remove the caramel from the pan in one piece. Place the caramel on a cutting board and use a sharp knife to cut the candy into 1-inch squares. If you wait until the caramel is cold, it will be difficult to cut.

7· If you're using candy molds, first pour the hot caramel into a Pyrex measuring cup with a handle and spout. This will make it easier to pour the caramel into the small molds. Slowly fill the molds just to the top. Let the caramels cool completely before popping them out of the molds, about 2 hours.

8· Wrap each caramel in wax paper and store them all in an airtight container at room temperature for up to 3 weeks.

VARIATIONS

CHOCOLATE ALMOND CARAMELS Add ½ teaspoon almond extract and ½ cup sliced almonds before pouring the hot caramel into the pan or molds.

CHOCOLATE COCONUT CARAMELS Add ½ cup shredded sweetened coconut before pouring the hot caramel into the pan or molds.

CHOCOLATE PEANUT CARAMELS Add ½ cup finely chopped salted peanuts before pouring the hot caramel into the pan or molds.

CHOCOLATE RASPBERRY CARAMELS Add 1 teaspoon natural or artificial raspberry flavoring before pouring the hot caramel into the pan or molds.

CHOCOLATE THAI CARAMELS Add 2 teaspoons crumbled dried basil and 1 teaspoon crushed red chili flakes with the chocolate.

CINNAMON CHOCOLATE CARAMELS Add 1 teaspoon ground cinnamon with the chocolate.

CHOCOLATE CHERRIES

This is perhaps one of the most delicious candies ever invented, and also one of the most clichéd—a firm chocolate shell surrounding a maraschino cherry swimming in a sweet, syrupy filling. The secret to the liquid center lies in dipping the cherries twice. The first dipping is into melted fondant. The fondant hardens and the cherries are dipped again into melted chocolate. The fondant will then reliquefy after the chocolate hardens. Magic!

3 cups sugar

1 cup plus 1 tablespoon water

¼ cup light corn syrup

60 maraschino cherries with stems
   (do not use fresh cherries)

24 ounces semisweet chocolate, roughly
   chopped, or 24 ounces semisweet
   chocolate chips

Butter or margarine for greasing the pan
   and the cookie sheet

1· **PREPARING THE FONDANT** Butter a 9 × 13-inch baking pan and set aside.

2· Combine the sugar, water, and corn syrup in a heavy medium saucepan. Using a wooden spoon, stir gently over medium heat until the sugar dissolves completely and the syrup comes to a boil.

3· Clip a candy thermometer to the inside of the pan and cook the syrup, without stirring, until it reaches 240°F (soft ball).

4· Immediately pour the hot syrup into the prepared 9 × 13-inch pan. Let the syrup cool undisturbed until the bottom of the pan feels lukewarm to the touch.

5· Using a heavy wooden spoon, stir the lukewarm mixture until it forms a ball. Some of this fondant may stick to the 9 × 13-inch pan. The fondant may also seize into a very hard ball that is impossible to stir. In any case, seal the ball of fondant into a 1-gallon plastic Ziploc bag, removing as much air from the bag as possible. Let the fondant rest 1 minute before continuing.

6· With the fondant sealed in the plastic bag, roll the candy with the heel of your hand, pressing down toward the counter. Continue this light kneading motion until the fondant looks smooth and creamy and feels like a firm cookie dough, about 10 minutes. Set the fondant aside, wrapped in plastic, while you prepare the cherries. The fondant can be made up to a week ahead of time and kept well wrapped in the refrigerator.

7· **FIRST DIPPING** Drain the cherries, reserving the liquid. Place the cherries on paper towels to absorb any excess liquid.

8· Butter a large cookie sheet. Line it with wax paper and set it aside.

9· Place the fondant in the top of a double boiler set over simmering water. If you don't have a double boiler, simply place the fondant in a medium bowl that fits snugly over a pot of simmering water. Stir the fondant until it melts. Rest a candy thermometer in the melted fondant and continue to stir gently, working around the thermometer, until the fondant reaches 150°F. Turn off the heat.

10· Stir in 2 or 3 tablespoons of the reserved cherry liquid to give the fondant a pink color and a mild cherry flavor. Should the fondant fall below 150°F, turn the heat on low and bring the water back to a simmer just until the temperature of the fondant rises back to 150°F.

11· To dip, hold one cherry by the stem and quickly dip it into the melted fondant to cover the cherry. Avoid getting fondant on the stem. Place the dipped cherry on the prepared cookie sheet. Repeat the process with the remaining cherries until all are dipped. Stir the fondant occasionally. If the fondant becomes too thick as you dip, add more cherry liquid, 1 tablespoon at a time, until a thinner consistency is reached. Set the dipped cherries aside while preparing the chocolate for dipping.

12· **SECOND DIPPING** Melt 12 ounces of the semisweet chocolate in the top of a clean double boiler set over hot water. If you don't have a double boiler, simply place the chocolate in a bowl that fits snugly over a pot of hot water.

13· When the chocolate has melted completely, remove the top part of the double boiler or the bowl from the hot water. Add the remaining 12 ounces of semisweet chocolate and stir until all of the chocolate is melted and smooth.

14· Insert a candy thermometer or chocolate thermometer into the melted chocolate. Its temperature should be 88 to 90°F. If the chocolate is too cold, place it back over the hot water until the temperature reaches 88 to 90°F. If it is too hot, let it cool until the desired temperature is reached.

15· Hold one fondant-covered cherry by the stem and dip it into the melted chocolate to cover the pink candy coating. Repeat the process with the remaining cherries until all are dipped. Stir the chocolate occasionally.

16· Let the cherries sit at room temperature for 2 hours. Place them in the refrigerator overnight, and the chocolate will harden while the centers liquefy.

17· Store the cherries in a single layer in an airtight container in the refrigerator for up to 2 weeks.

VARIATIONS

MILK CHOCOLATE CHERRIES Substitute 24 ounces milk chocolate for the semisweet chocolate.

WHITE CHOCOLATE CHERRIES Substitute 24 ounces white chocolate for the semisweet chocolate.

The following variations work with the base recipe or with either of the preceding chocolate variations.

NUTTY CHOCOLATE CHERRIES Place a small piece of toasted almond inside each cherry before dipping it into the melted fondant. If desired, also add ¼ teaspoon almond extract to the melted fondant before dipping the cherries.

SPICY CHOCOLATE CHERRIES Place a small piece of fresh jalapeño pepper inside each cherry before dipping it in the melted fondant.

SPIKED CHOCOLATE CHERRIES Drain the liquid from the jars of cherries. Refill the jars, covering the cherries with brandy, vodka, or kirsch. Let them soak for at least 24 hours. Substitute the soaking alcohol for the cherry liquid.

CHOCOLATE CHOCOLATE CREAMS

MAKES ABOUT 4 DOZEN LARGE CANDIES

We've all had them—rich chocolate cream candies—but most of us have no idea what to call the filling. It's not caramel; it's not nougat; it's not even fudge. It's fondant, a sweet, smooth paste that makes chocolate creams, well, chocolate *creams*. This is a recipe for chocolate fondant surrounded by a dark chocolate coating. It's a chocoholic's dream come true!

> 3 cups sugar
>
> 1½ cups water
>
> 6 tablespoons cocoa powder
>
> ⅓ cup light corn syrup
>
> ¼ teaspoon salt
>
> 24 ounces semisweet chocolate, coarsely chopped, or 24 ounces semisweet chocolate chips
>
> Butter or margarine for greasing the pan and the cookie sheet

1· Generously butter a 9 × 13-inch baking pan. Also butter a large cookie sheet and line it with wax paper. Set both aside.

2· **PREPARING THE FONDANT** Combine all the sugar, water, cocoa powder, corn syrup, and salt in a heavy, tall saucepan. Height is important because the cocoa will make the sugar syrup boil high in the pan. You'll have quite a mess if it spills over.

3· Place the pan over medium heat and stir until the sugar is completely dissolved and the syrup comes to a boil.

4· Clip a candy thermometer to the inside of the pan and cook the syrup, without stirring, until it reaches 240°F (soft ball).

5· Immediately pour the hot syrup into the prepared 9 × 13-inch pan. Let the syrup cool undisturbed until the bottom of the pan feels lukewarm to the touch.

6· Using a heavy wooden spoon, stir the lukewarm mixture until it forms a ball. Some of this fondant may stick to the 9 × 13-inch pan. The fondant may also seize into a very hard ball that is impossible to stir. In any case, seal the ball of fondant into a 1-gallon plastic Ziploc bag, removing as much air from the bag as possible. Let the fondant rest 1 minute before continuing.

7· With the fondant sealed in the plastic bag, roll the candy with the heel of your hand, pressing down toward the counter. Continue this light kneading motion until the fondant looks smooth and creamy and feels like a firm cookie dough, about 10 minutes. Shape bite-sized pieces of fondant into balls, squares, or rectangles. Place them on the prepared cookie sheet.

8· **DIPPING THE FONDANT** Melt 12 ounces of the semisweet chocolate in the top of a double boiler set over hot water. If you don't have a double boiler, simply place the chocolate in a bowl that fits snugly over a pot of hot water.

9· When the chocolate has melted completely, remove the top part of the double boiler or the bowl from the hot water. Add the remaining 12 ounces of semisweet chocolate and stir until all of the chocolate is melted and smooth.

10· Insert a candy thermometer or chocolate thermometer into the melted chocolate. Its temperature should be 88 to 90°F. If the chocolate is too cold, place it back over the hot water until the temperature reaches 88 to 90°F. If it is too hot, let it cool until the desired temperature is reached.

11· Spear each piece of fondant with a toothpick and dip it into the melted chocolate. Gently tap the toothpick on the edge of the bowl to remove any excess chocolate and place the candy back on the wax paper. The weight of the candy should release it from the toothpick. You can use the toothpick to add a drop of chocolate to cover the hole. Repeat with each piece of fondant, stirring the chocolate occasionally between dips. If your fondant centers fall off the toothpick into the chocolate, simply fish them out with a fork and gently tap off the extra chocolate, then flip them over onto the wax paper. Alternatively, use professional chocolate dipping tools. For advice on these, see page 3.

12· Let the chocolate chocolate creams sit uncovered at room temperature overnight. Store them in layers, separated by wax paper, in an airtight container at room temperature for up to 2 weeks.

MILK CHOCOLATE CHOCOLATE CREAMS Substitute 24 ounces milk chocolate for the semisweet chocolate.

WHITE CHOCOLATE CHOCOLATE CREAMS Substitute 24 ounces white chocolate for the semisweet chocolate.

The following variations work with the base recipe or with either of the preceding chocolate variations.

ALMOND CHOCOLATE CHOCOLATE CREAMS Add 1 teaspoon almond extract to the cooked syrup before pouring it into the prepared pan. If desired, wrap the fondant around a bite-sized piece of toasted almond before dipping it in the melted chocolate.

COCONUT CHOCOLATE CHOCOLATE CREAMS Add 2 teaspoons natural or artificial coconut flavoring to the cooked syrup before pouring it into the prepared pan. If desired, knead ¼ cup shredded coconut into the fondant before shaping it into balls, squares, or rectangles.

ORANGE CHOCOLATE CHOCOLATE CREAMS Add 2 teaspoons orange extract to the syrup before pouring it into the prepared pan. Knead 2 teaspoons grated orange rind into the fondant before shaping it into balls, squares, or rectangles.

PEPPERMINT PATTY CHOCOLATE CHOCOLATE CREAMS Add 2 to 3 teaspoons mint extract to the cooked syrup before pouring it into the prepared pan.

RUM CHOCOLATE CHOCOLATE CREAMS Add 1 tablespoon artificial rum flavoring to the syrup before pouring it into the prepared pan.

UNDIPPED CHOCOLATE CHOCOLATE CREAM CENTERS Fondant may also be shaped using candy molds and eaten plain, without being dipped in melted chocolate. See the Source Guide on page 242 for candy molds.

CHOCOLATE CREAMS

MAKES ABOUT 4 DOZEN LARGE CANDIES

These dipped chocolates are just like the ones that come in those heart-shaped boxes on Valentine's Day.

> 3 cups sugar
>
> 1 cup plus 1 tablespoon water
>
> ¼ cup light corn syrup
>
> 1 tablespoon vanilla extract
>
> 24 ounces semisweet chocolate, coarsely chopped, or 24 ounces semisweet chocolate chips
>
> Butter or margarine for greasing the pan and the cookie sheet

1· Generously butter a 9 × 13-inch baking pan. Butter a large cookie sheet and line with wax paper. Set both aside.

2· **PREPARING THE FONDANT** Combine the sugar, water, and corn syrup in a heavy medium saucepan and place it over medium heat. Stir until the sugar dissolves completely and the syrup comes to a boil.

3· Clip a candy thermometer to the inside of the pan and cook the syrup, without stirring, until it reaches 240°F (soft ball).

4· Immediately pour the hot syrup into the prepared 9 × 13-inch pan. Let the syrup cool undisturbed until the bottom of the pan feels lukewarm to the touch.

5· Add the vanilla and using a heavy wooden spoon, stir the lukewarm mixture until it forms a ball. Some of this fondant may stick to the 9 × 13-inch pan. The fondant may also seize into a very hard ball that is impossible to stir. In any case, seal the ball of fondant into a 1-gallon plastic Ziploc bag, removing as much air from the bag as possible. Let the fondant rest 1 minute before continuing.

6· With the fondant sealed in the plastic bag, roll the candy with the heel of your hand, pressing down toward the counter. Continue this light kneading motion until the fondant looks smooth and creamy and feels like a firm cookie dough, about 10 minutes. Shape bite-sized pieces of fondant into balls, squares, or rectangles. Place them on the prepared cookie sheet.

7· **DIPPING THE FONDANT** Melt 12 ounces of the semisweet chocolate in the top of a double boiler set over hot water. If you don't have a double boiler, simply place the chocolate in a bowl that fits snugly over a pot of hot water.

8· When the chocolate has melted completely, remove the top part of the double boiler or the bowl from the hot water. Add the remaining 12 ounces of semisweet chocolate and stir until all of the chocolate is melted and smooth.

9· Insert a candy thermometer or chocolate thermometer into the melted chocolate. Its temperature should be 88 to 90°F. If the chocolate is too cold, place it back over the hot water until the temperature reaches 88 to 90°F. If it is too hot, let it cool until the desired temperature is reached.

10· Spear each piece of fondant with a toothpick and dip it into the melted chocolate. Gently tap the toothpick on the edge of the bowl to remove any excess chocolate and place the candy back on the wax paper. The weight of the candy should release it from the toothpick. You can use the toothpick to add a drop of chocolate to cover the hole. Repeat with each piece of fondant, stirring the chocolate occasionally between dips. If your fondant centers fall off the toothpick into the chocolate, simply fish them out with a fork and gently tap off the extra chocolate, then flip them over onto the wax paper. Alternatively, use professional chocolate dipping tools. For advice on these, see page 3.

11· Let the chocolate creams sit uncovered at room temperature overnight. Store them in layers, separated by wax paper, in an airtight container at room temperature for up to 2 weeks.

VARIATIONS

BUTTERSCOTCH CHOCOLATE CREAMS Substitute 24 ounces butterscotch chips for the semisweet chocolate.

MILK CHOCOLATE CREAMS Substitute 24 ounces milk chocolate for the semisweet chocolate.

WHITE CHOCOLATE CREAMS Substitute 24 ounces white chocolate for the semisweet chocolate.

The following variations work with the base recipe or with any of the preceding variations.

ALMOND CHOCOLATE CREAMS Substitute 1 teaspoon almond extract for the vanilla extract. If desired, you may also wrap the fondant around a bite-sized piece of toasted almond before dipping it in the melted chocolate.

COCONUT CHOCOLATE CREAMS Substitute 1 tablespoon natural or artificial coconut flavoring for the vanilla extract. If desired, you may also knead ¼ cup shredded coconut into the fondant before shaping it into balls, squares, or rectangles.

LEMON CHOCOLATE CREAMS Substitute 1 tablespoon lemon extract for the vanilla extract. Knead 2 teaspoons grated lemon rind into the fondant before shaping it into balls, squares, or rectangles. If desired, you may also add 2 to 3 drops yellow food coloring.

ORANGE CHOCOLATE CREAMS Substitute 2 teaspoons orange extract for the vanilla extract. Knead 2 teaspoons grated orange rind into the fondant before shaping it into balls, squares, or rectangles. If desired, you may also add 2 to 3 drops orange food coloring.

PEPPERMINT PATTY CHOCOLATE CREAMS Substitute 2 teaspoons mint extract (not peppermint oil) for the vanilla extract.

RUM CHOCOLATE CREAMS Substitute 1 tablespoon artificial rum flavoring for the vanilla extract.

UNDIPPED CHOCOLATE CREAM CENTERS Fondant may also be shaped using candy molds and eaten plain, without being dipped in the melted chocolate. See the Source Guide on page 242 for candy molds.

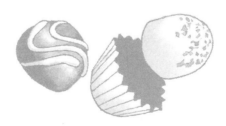

CHOCOLATE CREAMS DELUXE

While these candies are similar to regular Chocolate Creams (page 109), the centers are much richer because they contain both butter and cream.

> 2½ cups sugar
>
> 1 cup light cream
>
> 1 tablespoon light corn syrup
>
> ¼ teaspoon salt
>
> 3 tablespoons unsalted butter
>
> 1 tablespoon vanilla extract
>
> 24 ounces semisweet chocolate, chopped, or 24 ounces semisweet chocolate chips
>
> Butter or margarine for greasing the pan and the cookie sheet

1· Generously butter a 9 × 13-inch baking pan. Butter a large cookie sheet and line with wax paper. Set both aside.

2· **PREPARING THE FONDANT** Combine the sugar, cream, corn syrup, salt, and butter in a heavy tall-sided saucepan. Height is important as the cream will cause the sugar syrup to boil high in the pot. You'll have quite a mess if it boils over.

3· Place the pan over medium heat and stir until the sugar dissolves completely and the syrup comes to a boil.

4· Clip a candy thermometer to the inside of the pan and cook the syrup, without stirring, until it reaches 240°F (soft ball).

5· Immediately pour the hot syrup into the prepared 9 × 13-inch pan. Let the syrup cool undisturbed until the bottom of the pan feels lukewarm to the touch.

6· Add the vanilla, and using a heavy wooden spoon, stir the lukewarm mixture until it forms a ball. Some of this fondant may stick to the 9 × 13-inch pan. The fondant may also seize into a very hard ball that is impossible to stir. In any case, seal the ball of fondant into a 1-gallon plastic Ziploc bag, removing as much air from the bag as possible. Let the fondant rest 1 minute before continuing.

7· With the fondant sealed in the plastic bag, roll the candy with the heel of your hand, pressing down toward the counter. Continue this light kneading motion until the fondant looks smooth and creamy and feels like a firm cookie dough, about 10 minutes. Shape bite-sized pieces of fondant into balls, squares, or rectangles. Place them on the prepared cookie sheet.

8· **DIPPING THE FONDANT** Melt 12 ounces of the semisweet chocolate in the top of a double boiler set over hot water. If you don't have a double boiler, simply place the chocolate in a bowl that fits snugly over a pot of hot water.

9· When the chocolate has melted completely, remove the top part of the double boiler or the bowl from the hot water. Add the remaining 12 ounces of semisweet chocolate and stir until all of the chocolate is melted and smooth.

10· Insert a candy thermometer or chocolate thermometer into the melted chocolate. Its temperature should be 88 to 90°F. If the chocolate is too cold, place it back over the hot water until the temperature reaches 88 to 90°F. If it is too hot, let it cool until the desired temperature is reached.

11· Spear each piece of fondant with a toothpick and dip it into the melted chocolate. Gently tap the toothpick on the edge of the bowl to remove any excess chocolate and place the candy back on the wax paper. The weight of the candy should release it from the toothpick. You can use the toothpick to add a drop of chocolate to cover the hole. Repeat with each piece of fondant, stirring the chocolate occasionally between dips. If your fondant centers fall off the toothpick into the chocolate, simply fish them out with a fork and gently tap off the extra chocolate, then flip them over onto the wax paper. Alternatively, use professional chocolate dipping tools. For advice on these, see page 3.

12· Let the chocolate creams deluxe sit uncovered at room temperature overnight. Store them in layers, separated by wax paper, in an airtight container at room temperature for up to 2 weeks.

VARIATIONS

BUTTERSCOTCH CHOCOLATE CREAMS DELUXE Substitute 24 ounces butterscotch chips for the semisweet chocolate.

MILK CHOCOLATE CREAMS DELUXE Substitute 24 ounces milk chocolate for the semisweet chocolate.

WHITE CHOCOLATE CREAMS DELUXE Substitute 24 ounces white chocolate for the semisweet chocolate.

The following variations work with the base recipe or with any of the preceding variations.

BANANA CHOCOLATE CREAMS DELUXE Substitute 1 tablespoon natural or artificial banana flavoring for the vanilla extract.

CARAMEL CHOCOLATE CREAMS DELUXE Substitute 1 tablespoon natural or artificial caramel flavoring for the vanilla extract.

EARL GREY CHOCOLATE CREAMS DELUXE Omit the vanilla extract. Two hours before starting the recipe, warm the cream and add 4 Earl Grey tea bags. Let the tea steep in the cream until the cream is heavily scented with tea. Discard the tea bags.

LAVENDER CHOCOLATE CREAMS DELUXE Omit the vanilla extract. Two hours before starting the recipe, warm the cream and add 1 tablespoon dried lavender flowers. Let the flowers steep in the cream until the cream is heavily scented with lavender. Remove the flowers and discard. See the Source Guide on page 242 for dried lavender flowers.

MAPLE CHOCOLATE CREAMS DELUXE Substitute 1 tablespoon artificial maple flavoring for the vanilla extract.

RASPBERRY CHOCOLATE CREAMS DELUXE Substitute 1 tablespoon natural or artificial raspberry flavoring for the vanilla extract.

STRAWBERRY CHOCOLATE CREAMS DELUXE Substitute 1 tablespoon natural or artificial strawberry flavoring for the vanilla extract.

UNDIPPED CHOCOLATE CREAM DELUXE CENTERS Fondant may also be shaped using candy molds and eaten plain, without being dipped in melted chocolate. See the Source Guide on page 242 for candy molds.

CHOCOLATE DIVINITY

Divinity is usually white and creamy, a kind of candied meringue drop. But this version looks like chocolate whipped cream—and tastes like heaven on earth!

> 2 ounces unsweetened chocolate, coarsely chopped
>
> 3 large egg whites
>
> ¼ teaspoon salt
>
> 2 cups sugar
>
> ⅔ cup water
>
> ½ cup light corn syrup
>
> 2 teaspoons vanilla extract
>
> Butter or margarine for greasing the cookie sheet

1· Butter a large cookie sheet and line it with wax paper. Set aside.

2· Melt the chocolate in the top of a double boiler set over hot water, or in a bowl that fits snugly over a pan of hot water. When the chocolate has melted, remove the top from the double boiler or the bowl from the pan of hot water. Stir the chocolate until smooth, and set aside.

3· In a large mixing bowl, beat the egg whites and the salt with an electric mixer on high. When soft peaks form, set the bowl aside.

4· Combine the sugar, water, and corn syrup in a heavy medium saucepan. Place over medium heat and stir until the sugar is completely dissolved and the mixture comes to a boil.

5· Clip a candy thermometer to the inside of the pan. Raise the heat to medium-high and cook, without stirring, until the mixture reaches 260°F (hard ball). Remove the pan from the heat.

6· Turn the mixer back on and beat the egg whites for a few seconds to reincorporate any separation. With the beater running at high speed, slowly pour the hot syrup into the egg whites in a thin, steady stream. Beat until the divinity begins to lose its sheen and holds its shape when dropped from a spoon. Depending on the weather, this step can take anywhere from 5 to 15 minutes. Using a wooden spoon, quickly fold in the vanilla and the melted chocolate, until the chocolate is completely incorporated.

7· Drop by heaping tablespoonsful onto the prepared cookie sheet, spacing the drops ½ inch apart. When the divinity is cool and firm, peel it away from the wax paper and store it in an airtight container at room temperature for up to 1 week.

VARIATIONS

CHOCOLATE ALMOND DIVINITY Add 1½ cups slivered almonds with the vanilla and chocolate.

CHOCOLATE GINGER DIVINITY Add ¼ cup sliced fresh ginger to the pan with the sugar. Remove the ginger with a slotted spoon before pouring the hot syrup into the egg whites.

CHOCOLATE WALNUT DIVINITY Add 1½ cups chopped walnuts with the vanilla and chocolate.

DOUBLE CHOCOLATE DIVINITY Add 1 cup miniature chocolate chips with the vanilla and chocolate.

MEXICAN DIVINITY Add 1 teaspoon ground cinnamon to the egg whites before adding the sugar syrup. Then add ¼ teaspoon almond extract with the vanilla.

CHOCOLATE FUDGE

They say timing is everything. And it couldn't be more true than with fudge. Knowing just when to beat the mixture and when to stop is the key to a creamy candy that doesn't crystallize. Follow the recipe exactly and you should have perfect results: fudge that is quite firm, but melts in your mouth.

> 3 cups sugar
>
> 1 cup half-and-half
>
> 3 ounces unsweetened chocolate, coarsely chopped
>
> ¼ cup light corn syrup
>
> 3 tablespoons butter plus additional for greasing the pan
>
> ¼ teaspoon salt
>
> 2 teaspoons vanilla extract

1· Line a 10-inch square pan with wax paper, overhanging the edges by at least 2 inches. Butter the paper and set the pan aside.

2· Combine the sugar, half-and-half, chocolate, corn syrup, butter, and salt in a tall-sided heavy saucepan. Height is important, because the half-and-half will cause the syrup to boil high in the pan, and you don't want the syrup to boil over.

3· Stir over low heat until the sugar and chocolate are completely dissolved and the mixture comes to a boil.

4· Clip a candy thermometer to the inside of the pan. Raise the heat to medium and cook, without stirring, until the mixture reaches 236°F (just short of soft ball). Remove the pan from the heat and allow the mixture to cool undisturbed until the thermometer reads 110°F.

5· Add the vanilla and stir vigorously with a wooden spoon until the mixture loses its gloss and thickens to the consistency of cake icing. Using a buttered spatula, spread the mixture into the prepared pan and let it rest at room temperature for at least 6 hours.

6· When the fudge is firm, grab the edges of the wax paper and pull the candy out of the pan. Using a sharp knife, cut the fudge into bite-sized pieces. Store them in layers, separated by wax paper, in an airtight container at room temperature for up to 1 week.

VARIATIONS

CHOCOLATE CHERRY FUDGE Add 1 cup coarsely chopped dried cherries with the vanilla.

CHOCOLATE MARSHMALLOW FUDGE Add 1 cup mini marshmallows with the vanilla.

CHOCOLATE MEXICAN FUDGE Add 1 cup sliced almonds and ½ teaspoon ground cinnamon with the vanilla.

CHOCOLATE MINT FUDGE Add 1 cup lightly crushed peppermint candies with the vanilla.

CHOCOLATE PEANUT FUDGE Add 1 cup roasted, salted peanuts with the vanilla.

CHOCOLATE WALNUT FUDGE Add 1 cup coarsely chopped walnuts with the vanilla.

CHOCOLATE TAFFY

MAKES ABOUT 1 ½ POUNDS

This candy tastes and looks like Tootsie Rolls, only harder. And after a few moments in your mouth, this taffy softens nicely.

> 1½ cups sugar
> ½ cup cocoa powder
> ¼ teaspoon salt
> ¾ cup light corn syrup
> ¼ cup water
> 1 teaspoon white vinegar
> 1 tablespoon butter plus additional for
>   greasing the pan and the cookie sheet

1· **COOKING THE TAFFY** Generously butter a 9 × 13-inch baking pan and set it aside.

2· Combine the sugar, cocoa powder, and salt in a heavy medium saucepan. Stir until these dry ingredients are thoroughly combined. Add the corn syrup, water, and vinegar. Place the pan over medium heat. Stir until the sugar and cocoa are completely dissolved and the mixture comes to a boil.

3· Clip a candy thermometer to the inside of the pan and cook, without stirring, until the mixture reaches 260°F (hard ball).

4· Remove the pan from the heat and add the 1 tablespoon butter. Stir until the butter melts. Pour the hot syrup into the prepared 9 × 13-inch pan and allow it to cool until the bottom of the pan feels warm, but not hot. The taffy will still be soft and slightly runny, and is now ready to be pulled.

5· **PULLING THE TAFFY** Butter a large cookie sheet (preferably nonstick) or butter a large marble slab. If you have a marble or granite counter, by all means use it. Simply clean it, then generously butter it.

6· Pour the warm candy onto the prepared work surface. Lightly butter your hands and start folding the taffy onto itself by taking the corners and bringing them up onto the middle of the taffy. Continue folding the corners back onto the center until the taffy can be gathered into a ball, about 3 minutes. The taffy is now ready to be pulled. If your hands are small, you may prefer to divide this ball of taffy into 2 or 3 pieces before you begin to pull the candy.

7· Holding the ball of taffy with both hands, pull it into a rope about 2 feet long, twisting the rope as you pull. Bring the ends of the rope together, creating a shorter, 1-foot rope. Pull this 1-foot rope of taffy to a length of 2 feet or more, twisting the rope as you pull. Bring the ends together again. Repeat this process until the taffy becomes light brown and is very hard to pull, about 10 minutes.

8· Divide the pulled taffy into 4 pieces. Roll or pull each piece into a rope about ½ inch in diameter. Cut each rope into bite-sized pieces with buttered scissors.

9· Wrap the cooled taffy pieces individually in wax paper and store them all in an airtight container at room temperature for up to 3 weeks.

VARIATIONS

ALMOND CHOCOLATE TAFFY Add ½ teaspoon almond extract and ¾ cup chopped toasted slivered almonds with the butter. For advice on toasting almonds, see page 12.

COCONUT CHOCOLATE TAFFY Add ¾ cup shredded coconut with the butter.

MOCHA TAFFY Add 1 tablespoon instant espresso powder with the sugar and cocoa powder.

PEANUT CHOCOLATE TAFFY Add ¾ cup chopped salted peanuts with the butter.

SOFT CHOCOLATE TAFFY Remove the pan from the heat when the temperature reaches 255°F (between firm ball and hard ball).

COCOA MERINGUE KISSES

These are bite-sized chocolate sweets that are baked like cookies in a very low-temperature oven. As with all egg white–based confections, you will have better results if you make these on a bright, clear day with low humidity.

> 2 large egg whites
> ¼ teaspoon salt
> ¼ teaspoon cream of tartar
> 1¼ cups superfine sugar
> ¼ cup cocoa powder, sifted
> Butter or margarine for greasing the cookie
>   sheets

1· Preheat the oven to 180°F. Butter two large cookie sheets and line them with parchment paper. Set the sheets aside.

2· In a medium mixing bowl, beat the egg whites and salt with an electric mixer on high until they are foamy. Add the cream of tartar and continue to beat until soft peaks form. Beat in the sugar a few tablespoons at a time. Continue beating until you no longer feel any sugar when you rub a little of the mixture between your fingers. Beat in the cocoa powder until it is completely incorporated.

3· Drop by tablespoonsful onto the prepared cookie sheets. Leave a little peak at the top of each one to resemble a chocolate kiss.

4· Bake for 1½ hours. Turn off the heat, prop the oven door open, and allow the kisses to cool completely in the oven.

5· Peel the cooled kisses off the parchment and store them in airtight containers at room temperature for up to 2 weeks.

VARIATIONS

ALMOND CHOCOLATE MERINGUE KISSES Add ½ teaspoon almond extract and ½ cup sliced almonds with the cocoa.

CHOCOLATE CHIP CHOCOLATE MERINGUE KISSES Add ½ cup miniature chocolate chips with the cocoa.

CINNAMON CHOCOLATE MERINGUE KISSES Add ½ teaspoon ground cinnamon with the cocoa.

WHITE CHOCOLATE CHOCOLATE MERINGUE KISSES Add ½ cup white chocolate chips with the cocoa.

COCONUT MOUNDS

These bite-sized versions of Mounds bars are even better than the original because you make them yourself with the finest-quality chocolate.

¾ cup light corn syrup

½ cup sugar

¼ cup water

2 heaping cups shredded sweetened coconut

12 ounces semisweet chocolate, coarsely chopped, or 12 ounces semisweet chocolate chips

Butter or margarine for greasing the cookie sheet

1· Butter a large cookie sheet and line it with wax paper. Butter the paper and set the sheet aside.

2· Combine the corn syrup, sugar, and water in a heavy medium saucepan. Place the pan over medium heat. Stir until the sugar dissolves completely and the mixture comes to a boil.

3· Clip a candy thermometer to the inside of the pan and cook until the syrup reaches 240°F (soft ball). Add the coconut and continue cooking, stirring constantly until the mixture reaches 248°F (firm ball).

4· Remove the pan from the heat. Pour the mixture into a heatproof bowl and set it aside to cool completely, about 4 hours. Refrigerate the mixture for at least 2 hours to chill, making it easier to handle.

5· Use your fingers to pinch off 1 tablespoon of the mixture and shape it into a small rectangle. Place the rectangle on the prepared cookie sheet and repeat the process with the remaining coconut mixture. Place the coconut rectangles in the refrigerator until you are ready to dip them in the melted chocolate.

6· Melt 6 ounces of the semisweet chocolate in the top of a double boiler set over hot water. If you don't have a double boiler, simply place the chocolate in a bowl that fits snugly over a pot of hot water.

7· When the chocolate has melted completely, remove the top part of the double boiler or the bowl from the hot water. Add the remaining 6 ounces of semisweet chocolate and stir until all of the chocolate is melted and smooth.

8· Insert a candy thermometer or chocolate thermometer into the melted chocolate. Its temperature should be 88 to 90°F. If the chocolate is too cold, place it back over the hot water until the temperature reaches 88 to 90°F. If it is too hot, let it cool until the desired temperature is reached.

9· To dip the coconut centers, place one center onto a fork with narrow tines. Dip the coconut center into the chocolate and lift it out. Tap the fork on the edge of the chocolate pot or bowl to remove any excess chocolate.

10· Carefully slide the chocolate-covered coconut rectangle off the fork and back onto the cookie sheet. Repeat the process with the remaining coconut centers. Alternatively, use professional dipping tools instead of a fork. For advice on them, see page 3.

11· Allow the chocolate-dipped coconut mounds to rest at room temperature for 4 hours, for the chocolate to harden. The cooler your room's temperature, the faster the chocolate will set. You can speed up the process by placing them back in the refrigerator for 10 minutes, but no longer. If you don't mind a dull finish on your chocolate, you can let the candies cool completely in the refrigerator. They are especially delicious cold, or even frozen.

12· Store the coconut mounds in an airtight container in layers, separated by wax paper, at room temperature for up to 1 week, in the refrigerator for up to 3 weeks, or in the freezer for up to 3 months.

VARIATIONS

MILK CHOCOLATE COCONUT MOUNDS Substitute 12 ounces milk chocolate for the semisweet chocolate.

WHITE CHOCOLATE COCONUT MOUNDS Substitute 12 ounces white chocolate for the semisweet chocolate.

The following variations work with the base recipe or with either of the preceding chocolate variations.

ALMOND COCONUT MOUNDS Press a whole almond onto the top of the coconut rectangle before dipping it in the melted chocolate.

CHERRY COCONUT MOUNDS Press a whole candied cherry onto the top of the coconut rectangle before dipping it in the melted chocolate.

DATE ROLLS

Esther Lou Scarbrough from Dallas, Texas, taught me how to make this rich and chewy fruit candy. She made it for her boys every Christmas for thirty years. The first time I tried it I knew how lucky her kids were. If you think dates are rich on their own, just wait until you try them rolled up into this sweet confection.

> 2½ cups sugar
>
> 1 cup milk
>
> 1 tablespoon light corn syrup
>
> ¼ teaspoon salt
>
> 3 tablespoons unsalted butter
>
> 2 teaspoons vanilla extract
>
> 2 cups finely chopped dried dates

1· Combine the sugar, milk, corn syrup, and salt in a heavy, tall saucepan. Height is important because the milk will cause the sugar syrup to boil high in the pot. You'll have quite a mess if it spills over.

2· Place the pan over medium heat. Stir until the sugar is completely dissolved and the mixture comes to a boil.

3· Clip a candy thermometer to the inside of the pan. Raise the heat to high and cook the syrup, without stirring, until it reaches 238°F (just short of soft ball).

4· Remove the pan from the heat and add the butter without stirring. Allow the mixture to cool undisturbed until the thermometer reads 110°F.

5· Add the vanilla and the dates all at once and beat the mixture with a wooden spoon until it forms a ball. Turn the mixture onto a cutting board or the counter and knead it with the heels of your hands until it's firm and smooth.

6· Divide the candy into 4 pieces and roll each piece into a log about 1½ inches in diameter. Wrap each log in plastic wrap and place them in the refrigerator to ripen for at least 24 hours. The date rolls will keep, wrapped, in the refrigerator for up to 1 week.

7· To serve, slice the logs into ½-inch disks and serve them at room temperature.

VARIATIONS

ALMOND DATE BALLS Instead of logs, shape the candy into 1-inch balls and roll each one in finely chopped almonds before refrigerating.

APRICOT DATE ROLLS Reduce the amount of chopped dates to 1 cup. Add 1 cup finely chopped dried apricots with the remaining dates.

COCONUT DATE ROLLS Roll each log in shredded sweetened coconut before refrigerating.

FIG DATE ROLLS Reduce the amount of chopped dates to 1 cup. Add 1 cup finely chopped dried figs with the remaining dates.

PECAN DATE BALLS Instead of logs, shape the candy into 1-inch balls and roll each one in finely chopped pecans before refrigerating.

WALNUT DATE ROLLS Reduce the amount of chopped dates to 1 cup. Add 1 cup finely chopped walnuts with the remaining dates.

DIVINITY

If I had to rename divinity, I would call it *candy meringue*. It's simply egg whites, cooked by the heat of boiling sugar syrup, with vanilla added. When it works, divinity is light and airy. But humid weather can make things difficult. Pick a clear, high-pressure day, use fresh eggs, and you should always have success.

> 2 large egg whites
> ¼ teaspoon salt
> 2½ cups sugar
> ½ cup water
> ½ cup light corn syrup
> 1 tablespoon vanilla extract
> Butter or margarine for greasing the cookie
>   sheet

1· Butter a large cookie sheet and line it with wax paper. Set aside.

2· In a large mixing bowl, beat the egg whites and the salt with an electric mixer on high. When soft peaks form, set the bowl aside.

3· Combine the sugar, water, and corn syrup in a heavy medium saucepan. Place over medium heat and stir until the sugar is completely dissolved and the mixture comes to a boil.

4· Clip a candy thermometer to the inside of the pan. Raise the heat to medium-high and cook, without stirring, until the mixture reaches 260°F (hard ball). Remove the pan from the heat.

5· Turn the mixer back on and beat the egg whites for a few seconds to reincorporate any separation. With the beater running at high speed, slowly pour the hot syrup into the egg whites in a thin, steady stream. Beat until the divinity begins to lose its sheen and holds its shape when dropped from a spoon. Depending on the weather, this step can take anywhere from 5 to 15 minutes. Quickly beat in the vanilla.

6· Drop by heaping tablespoonsful onto the prepared cookie sheet, spacing the drops ½ inch apart. When the divinity is cool and firm, peel it away from the wax paper and store it in an airtight container at room temperature for up to 1 week.

VARIATIONS

BLACK BOTTOM DIVINITY Dip the bottoms of the finished divinity into melted chocolate chips and then place back on clean wax paper until the chocolate has set up. (For advice on melting chocolate, see page 11.)

CHRISTMAS DIVINITY Add 1 cup chopped red and green candied cherries with the vanilla.

FLORIDA DIVINITY Add 1 teaspoon lemon extract and ¾ cup chopped candied citron with the vanilla.

HALLOWEEN DIVINITY Spoon the divinity out as directed and immediately dust each mound with orange and black sugar or sprinkles. Alternatively, add 5 drops orange or black food coloring with the vanilla.

NEW ENGLAND DIVINITY Add 1 cup coarsely chopped walnuts and ½ cup whole dried cranberries with the vanilla.

PINK MINT DIVINITY Substitute ½ teaspoon mint extract and 2 drops red food color for the vanilla. If desired, you may also add 1 cup crushed peppermint candies with the mint extract.

TEXAS DIVINITY Add 1 cup coarsely chopped pecans with the vanilla.

GRANOLA CHEWY BARS

These granola bars are dense and thick. Redolent with honey and maple, they're perfect served plain or dipped in chocolate. Use store-bought or homemade granola and *real* maple syrup.

1½ cups sugar
½ cup water
½ cup corn syrup
½ cup honey
½ cup real maple syrup
1 teaspoon vanilla extract
7 cups granola cereal
Vegetable oil for greasing the pan
Confectioners' sugar for coating

1· Oil a 9 × 13-inch Pyrex baking pan and set it aside.

2· Combine the sugar, water, corn syrup, honey, and maple syrup in a heavy medium saucepan. Place the pan over medium heat. Stir until the sugar is dissolved and the mixture comes to a boil.

3· Clip a candy thermometer to the inside of the pan. Raise the heat to medium-high and cook, without stirring, until the mixture reaches 250°F (firm ball).

4· Remove the pan from the heat and add the vanilla and granola all at once. Stir until the cereal is thoroughly incorporated. Spread the hot mixture into the prepared 9 × 13-inch pan. Set it aside on a cooling rack until the bottom of the pan feels cool.

5· Use a sharp knife to cut the cooled granola mixture into bars while it is still in the pan. Lift each bar out with a spatula and wrap them individually in wax paper. If the granola bars are too sticky to handle, you may coat them with confectioners' sugar before wrapping.

6· Store them at room temperature in an airtight container for up to 2 weeks.

CRANBERRY CASHEW GRANOLA BARS Reduce the amount of granola to 5 cups. Add 1 cup whole dried cranberries and 1 cup coarsely chopped toasted cashews with the cereal. For advice on toasting nuts, see page 12.

GOLDEN ALMOND COCONUT GRANOLA BARS Reduce the amount of granola to 5 cups. Add 1 cup unsweetened coconut chips, ½ cup golden raisins, and ½ cup slivered almonds with the cereal.

HOT PUMPKIN SEED GRANOLA BARS Reduce the amount of granola to 5 cups. Add 2 cups shelled, toasted pumpkin seeds and 1 tablespoon ground ancho chili powder with the granola. For advice on toasting pumpkin seeds, see page 233.

RAISIN NUT GRANOLA BARS Reduce the amount of granola to 5 cups. Add 1 cup raisins and 1 cup salted peanuts with the cereal.

TROPICAL GRANOLA BARS Reduce the amount of granola to 5 cups. Add 1 cup unsweetened coconut chips and 1 cup coarsely chopped dried papaya with the cereal.

GUMMY BEARS

These gummy bears are softer than the store-bought variety. And they require a candy mold. For bears, other animals, or fruit-shaped molds, see the Source Guide on page 242.

1 box (1¾ ounces) powdered pectin (available in many supermarkets or hardware stores)

½ teaspoon baking soda

¾ cup water

1 cup light corn syrup

1 cup granulated sugar

2 teaspoons lemon extract or orange extract

6 to 8 drops yellow or orange food coloring (optional)

Vegetable oil for coating the molds

Superfine sugar for coating the candy

1· Lightly oil enough candy molds to make 36 medium-size bears. Set them aside.

2· Combine the pectin and baking soda in a heavy medium saucepan. Add the water and place the pan over medium heat. Stir well until the pectin is dissolved. The mixture will foam as it heats. Continue to cook, stirring constantly, until the mixture is thick, smooth, and clear, 2 to 3 minutes. Turn off the heat and cover the pan to keep the pectin warm.

3· Combine the corn syrup and granulated sugar in another heavy medium saucepan. Place the pan over high heat. Stir until the sugar dissolves and the mixture comes to a boil.

4· Clip a candy thermometer to the inside of the pan. Cook, without stirring, until the mixture reaches 260°F (hard ball). Immediately add the pectin mixture and return the syrup to a boil. Boil exactly 1 minute and remove the pan from the heat.

5· Add the lemon or orange flavoring, the corresponding food coloring, and mix until thoroughly incorporated. Pour the syrup into the prepared molds and set them aside at room temperature until the candy has cooled and firmed up, about 5 hours.

6· While the candies are still in their molds, sprinkle the tops of the candies with superfine sugar. The candy is very sticky and the sugar will allow you to handle the candies and remove them from the molds. Shake off any excess sugar and use your fingers to peel the gummy bears out of the molds. Completely cover each bear with additional superfine sugar. Shake off the excess sugar and store the candies in an airtight container at room temperature for up to 1 week.

VARIATIONS

GUMMY FRUITS Use fruit-shaped molds and substitute 2 teaspoons of the corresponding natural or artificial fruit flavors (such as peach, strawberry, raspberry, apple, cassis, coconut, banana, and apricot) for the lemon or orange extract. Change the food coloring accordingly. For candy flavorings, see the Source Guide on page 242.

LICORICE GUMMY CANDY Omit the orange or lemon extract and food colorings. Add 2 teaspoons natural or artificial anise flavoring and pour the syrup into plain round molds. If desired, 4 drops of black food coloring can be added.

SOUR GUMMY CANDY Add ¼ teaspoon citric acid to the pan with the sugar and corn syrup.

SUPER SOUR GUMMY CANDY Mix 2 teaspoons citric acid with each ½ cup superfine sugar used for coating the finished candy.

HALLOWEEN CANDY

MAKES ABOUT 1 ½ POUNDS

This candy has the consistency of candy corn. Shape it by hand into little corn kernels or use molds to form ghosts, bats, witches, or pumpkins. For all candy molds, see the Source Guide on page 242.

2½ cups confectioners' sugar

⅓ cup nonfat dry milk

½ teaspoon salt

1 cup granulated sugar

⅔ cup light corn syrup

6 tablespoons unsalted butter

2 teaspoons vanilla

4 to 5 drops food coloring (orange, yellow, brown, or black)

1· Combine the confectioners' sugar, dry milk, and salt in a medium bowl. Mix well and set aside.

2· Combine the granulated sugar, corn syrup, and butter in a heavy large saucepan and place over medium heat. Stir until the butter melts and the sugar dissolves completely. Raise the heat to high and boil the syrup for 5 minutes, stirring constantly.

3· Remove the pan from the heat and stir in the vanilla and food coloring. Add the prepared dry ingredients and stir with a wooden spoon until the mixture forms a ball. When cool enough to handle, turn the ball onto the counter or a cutting board. Knead the ball using the heels of your hands until it has the consistency of a firm cookie dough.

4· Break off small pieces and press them into candy molds. The candies will release from the molds when they're turned upside down. The candies will also hold their shape as they cool. Alternatively, break off small pieces of the candy and mold them by hand into any shape desired.

VARIATIONS

CHRISTMAS CANDY Shape candy into winter holiday shapes and use red, green, white, silver, or gold food coloring. Winter molds include snowmen, Santas, nutcracker soldiers, reindeer, or angels.

EASTER CANDY Shape candy into spring holiday shapes and use pink, yellow, light blue, pastel green, and lavender food coloring. Spring molds include bunnies, flowers, eggs, baskets, or hearts.

HALVAH

Halvah is a Middle Eastern sweet made from sesame oil and a paste of ground sesame seeds called tahini. Tahini and sesame oil can be found in many supermarkets, health food stores, gourmet stores, or shops that sell Mediterranean specialties. When you shop for sesame oil, you will find toasted and untoasted varieties. I prefer the untoasted variety for this recipe. You can use toasted sesame oil, but the flavor will be very strong. While commercial halvah is often found in large wheels that resemble cheese and is sold by the pound, in this recipe the halvah is formed in a small loaf pan and sliced into pieces before serving.

½ cup untoasted sesame oil
2 cups all-purpose flour
1 cup tahini
¾ cup honey

1· Warm the oil in a large heavy skillet over low heat. Add the flour and stir until the oil and flour are thoroughly combined. Continue cooking, stirring occasionally, until the mixture begins to turn pale brown. Add the tahini and stir until the mixture has a uniform color and consistency. Turn off the heat.

2· In a separate small saucepan, bring the honey to a boil over high heat. Boil for 1 minute. Immediately add the hot honey to the flour mixture. Stir until the honey is completely incorporated.

3· Spread the mixture into a small ungreased 5 × 9-inch loaf pan and pack the mixture down with the back of a spatula. Let the halvah cool at room temperature for at least 2 hours or until the pan feels cool. The halvah will shrink back slightly from the edges of the pan as it cools, and should therefore unmold easily when the pan is inverted. Wrap the halvah in plastic wrap and store it in the refrigerator for up to 2 weeks.

4· To serve, cut the halvah into thin slices.

VARIATIONS

ALMOND HALVAH Add ½ cup slivered, toasted almonds with the honey. For advice on toasting nuts, see page 12.

CHOCOLATE HALVAH Place half the halvah into the loaf pan and cover with a layer of semisweet chocolate chips, about ⅓ cup. Cover with the remaining halvah and pack it down with the back of a spatula.

DOUBLE SESAME HALVAH Add ½ cup toasted sesame seeds with the honey. For advice on toasting sesame seeds, see page 12.

PISTACHIO HALVAH Add ½ cup whole shelled pistachio nuts with the honey.

ICEBOX DIVINITY

This particular divinity runs like ripe Brie when left at room temperature. So store it in the refrigerator and serve it cold, or at room temperature, spooned over ice cream, fruit, or nuts.

2 large egg whites

2½ cups sugar

1½ cups light corn syrup

¾ cup water

¼ teaspoon salt

2 teaspoons vanilla extract

Butter or margarine for greasing the pan

Confectioners' sugar for dusting the buttered pan

1· Butter a 9 × 13-inch baking pan and sprinkle it with confectioners' sugar. Shake off any excess sugar and set the pan aside.

2· Beat the egg whites in a large bowl with an electric mixer until they are stiff but not dry. Set aside.

3· Combine the sugar, corn syrup, water, and salt in a heavy saucepan. Place the pan over medium heat. Stir until the sugar dissolves completely and the mixture comes to a boil.

4· Clip a candy thermometer to the inside of the pan. Raise the heat to medium-high and cook the syrup, without stirring, until it reaches 240°F (soft ball). Do not turn off the heat.

5· Ladle 1 cup of hot syrup out of the pan and transfer it to a Pyrex measuring cup with a handle and spout. On medium speed, beat this sugar syrup into the egg whites, pouring it in a thin stream. Continue to beat the egg whites on medium speed while the remaining syrup boils. Boil the remaining syrup until it reaches 250°F (firm ball).

6· Remove the pan from the heat and slowly pour the remaining syrup into the egg-white mixture on medium speed. Beat until the egg-white mixture is very thick and the bowl is just warm to the touch. At this point, the divinity should still have a hint of gloss. Beat in the vanilla extract.

7· Spread the thick divinity mixture into the prepared pan and set it in the refrigerator to cool completely, at least 2 hours. Cut the divinity into thin slices while it is still in the pan. Remove the slices with a narrow spatula and serve them cold. Alternatively, you can leave the cooled divinity at room temperature and spoon it onto plates along with nuts and fruit.

VARIATIONS

CRANBERRY ORANGE ICEBOX DIVINITY Add 1 teaspoon orange extract and 1½ cups dried cranberries with the vanilla.

OREO CRUNCH ICEBOX DIVINITY Beat 2 cups crumbled Oreo cookies into the divinity with the vanilla.

PECAN ICEBOX DIVINITY Beat 1½ cups chopped pecans into the divinity with the vanilla.

TURKISH ICEBOX DIVINITY Add 1 cup shelled pistachios and 1 cup finely chopped dried apricots with the vanilla.

INFUSED TRUFFLES

Infusing the cream with herbs, teas, and other flavors is a versatile way to flavor truffles. Maison du Chocolat in Paris and New York has a wide variety of truffles prepared in this manner. Now you can make them without paying $75 a pound!

> 16 ounces semisweet chocolate, coarsely chopped, or 16 ounces semisweet chocolate chips
>
> ¾ cup heavy cream
>
> 3 tablespoons black tea leaves
>
> 3 tablespoons unsalted butter, at room temperature
>
> ½ cup cocoa powder, for coating

1· Place the chocolate in a medium mixing bowl and set aside.

2· Place the cream and tea leaves in a small saucepan and set it over low heat. Warm the cream until small bubbles appear around the edge of the pan and the cream begins to give off a little steam. Remove the pan from the heat, cover, and set the cream aside to steep for at least 30 minutes.

3· Strain the tea leaves from the cream and return the cream to a simmer over low heat. Turn off the heat and pour the hot cream over the chopped chocolate. Stir until the chocolate melts and the mixture is completely smooth. Add the butter and stir until well incorporated.

4· Place the mixture in the refrigerator for an hour, or until it is firm enough to shape into balls.

5· Scoop out a heaping teaspoonful of the chocolate mixture and roll it into a ball between your palms. Roll the ball in cocoa until it is completely covered. Roll it lightly in your palms again to make sure the cocoa sticks, then reroll the truffle in the cocoa. Repeat with the remaining chocolate mixture. If the mixture gets too soft to hold its shape, place it back in the refrigerator for 10 minutes, or until it can be handled easily.

6. Store the truffles in layers, separated by wax paper, in an airtight container in the refrigerator for up to 2 weeks. However, they are best served at room temperature.

VARIATIONS

SEMISWEET CHOCOLATE INFUSED TRUFFLES Dip the shaped truffles into melted dark chocolate instead of rolling them in cocoa. (For advice on melting chocolate, see page 11.) You will need about 16 ounces of melted semisweet chocolate for 24 truffles.

WHITE CHOCOLATE INFUSED TRUFFLES Dip the shaped truffles into melted white chocolate instead of rolling them in cocoa powder. (For advice on melting chocolate, see page 11.) You will need about 16 ounces of melted white chocolate for 24 truffles.

The following variations work with the base recipe or with either of the preceding chocolate variations.

BASIL TRUFFLES Substitute ¼ cup packed basil leaves, shredded, for the black tea leaves.

COFFEE TRUFFLES Substitute ½ cup whole coffee beans for the black tea leaves.

EARL GREY TRUFFLES Substitute 3 tablespoons Earl Grey tea leaves for the black tea leaves.

GINGER TRUFFLES Substitute ¼ cup thinly sliced peeled ginger for the black tea leaves.

JUNIPER TRUFFLES Substitute 3 tablespoons juniper berries for the black tea leaves. If desired, you may also add 2 tablespoons gin with the butter.

TARRAGON TRUFFLES Substitute 3 tablespoons fresh tarragon leaves for the black tea leaves.

LEMONADE JELLIES

MAKES ABOUT 1 POUND

These are little square jelly candies that taste just like fresh lemonade. With a fine sugar coating, they are sweet on the outside and tart on in the inside. Use only freshly squeezed lemon juice for true lemonade flavor.

> 3 envelopes unflavored gelatin
> 1 cup water
> 2 cups granulated sugar
> ¾ cup fresh lemon juice
> 1 teaspoon grated fresh lemon rind
> Vegetable oil for coating the pan
> Superfine sugar for coating the candy

1· Oil an 8-inch square pan. Set aside.

2· In a small bowl, sprinkle the gelatin over ½ cup water. Let the gelatin soften at room temperature for 5 minutes.

3· Meanwhile, combine the remaining ½ cup water and the granulated sugar in a heavy medium saucepan. Place the pan over medium heat. Stir until the sugar dissolves completely and the mixture comes to a boil.

4· Clip a candy thermometer to the inside of the pan and cook, without stirring, until the syrup reaches 260°F (hard ball). Remove the pan from the heat.

5· Add the gelatin to the hot syrup and stir until it is completely dissolved. Stir in the lemon juice and rind.

6· Pour the syrup into the prepared pan. Cool at room temperature until the candy is set, at least 3 hours.

7· Cover the top of the candy with superfine sugar. Invert the pan and gently remove the candy in one piece, placing it sugared-side down on a cutting board. Using a wet knife, cut the candy into 1-inch squares. Coat each square with additional superfine sugar. Store the jellies in an airtight container in layers, separated by wax paper, at room temperature for up to 1 week.

VARIATIONS

COCONUT LEMONADE JELLIES Add ½ teaspoon natural or artificial coconut flavoring with the lemon juice.

EXTRA-SOUR LEMONADE JELLIES Add ¼ teaspoon citric acid with the lemon juice.

LIMEADE JELLIES Substitute ¾ cup fresh lime juice and 1 teaspoon grated fresh lime rind for the lemon juice and lemon rind.

PINK LEMONADE JELLIES Add 1 tablespoon grenadine syrup with the lemon juice.

MAPLE FUDGE

This soft nonchocolate fudge is best kept in the refrigerator and served cold. Use only real maple syrup to make the fudge—pancake syrup will not work.

> 2 cups real maple syrup
>
> ¾ cup half-and-half
>
> 2 tablespoons light corn syrup
>
> ⅛ teaspoon salt
>
> 1 tablespoon unsalted butter plus additional
>   for greasing the paper
>
> 2 teaspoons vanilla extract

1· Line a 10-inch square pan with wax paper, overlapping the edges at least 2 inches. Butter the paper and set the pan aside.

2· Combine the maple syrup, half-and-half, corn syrup, and salt in a heavy tall-sided saucepan. Height is important because the half-and-half will cause the sugar syrup to boil high in the pan, and you don't want the syrup to boil over.

3· Place the pan over medium heat. Stir until the sugar is completely dissolved and the mixture comes to a boil.

4· Clip a candy thermometer to the inside of the pan and cook without stirring until it reaches 240°F (soft ball).

5· Remove the pan from the heat and allow the mixture to cool undisturbed until the thermometer reads 110°F.

6· Add the butter and vanilla all at once. Stir vigorously with a wooden spoon until the mixture loses its gloss and thickens to the consistency of cake icing. Using a buttered spatula, spread the mixture into the prepared pan and place it in the refrigerator to cool for at least 8 hours.

7· Grab the edges of the wax paper and pull the candy out of the pan. Using a sharp knife, cut the fudge into bite-sized pieces. Store them in layers, separated by wax paper, in the refrigerator for up to 1 week.

VARIATIONS

MAPLE ALMOND FUDGE Add 1 cup chopped toasted almonds and ½ teaspoon almond extract with the vanilla. For advice on toasting nuts, see page 12.

MAPLE BANANA CRUNCH FUDGE Add 1 cup crumbled banana chips with the vanilla.

MAPLE COFFEE FUDGE Dissolve 1 tablespoon instant espresso powder in 1 tablespoon water and add it to the pan with the maple syrup.

MAPLE PECAN FUDGE Add 1 cup chopped pecans with the vanilla.

MAPLE RAISIN FUDGE Add 1 cup golden raisins with the vanilla.

MAPLE WALNUT FUDGE Add 1 cup chopped walnuts with the vanilla.

MARRONS GLACÉS

This is a traditional French confection—preserved, sweet chestnuts. They are more popular at Christmas but can be found year round. The easiest way to tackle this time-consuming candy is to use dried chestnuts instead of fresh. They'll still take five days to make, but since the chestnuts are already peeled, your job will be much easier. For a truly American version of this French sweet, try the variations using squash or pumpkin. Look for dried chestnuts at your local health food store or consult the Source Guide on page 242.

> 3 cups dried chestnuts
> 1 cup granulated sugar
> 1 cup dark brown sugar
> 1 vanilla bean, split

1· Place the chestnuts in a large bowl and cover them with water to a depth of 4 inches. Cover the bowl with a towel and let it stand overnight.

2· Drain the chestnuts and place them in a heavy medium saucepan with 3 cups of water. Bring the water to a simmer over medium heat and cook for 15 to 20 minutes, or until the chestnuts are just tender when pierced with the tip of a knife.

3· Remove the chestnuts with a slotted spoon and place them in a large bowl. Add the granulated sugar, brown sugar, and vanilla bean to the water remaining in the pan and stir until the sugars dissolve completely. Bring the mixture to a boil and immediately pour the hot syrup over the chestnuts. Let the chestnuts cool in the syrup overnight.

4· Drain the chestnuts from the syrup with a slotted spoon and bring the syrup back to a boil over high heat. Once again, pour the hot syrup over the chestnuts and let them cool in the syrup overnight.

5· Repeat this process for 2 more days.

6· Discard the vanilla bean. Remove the chestnuts from the syrup and place them on a wire rack at least ½ inch apart to dry, about 6 hours. When they are just slightly sticky to the touch, wrap each piece in wax paper and store them in an airtight container at room temperature for up to 1 week.

VARIATIONS

CHESTNUTS IN SYRUP Do not remove the chestnuts from the syrup after the final cooling. Store the chestnuts in the syrup and serve in a small bowl with a little unsweetened whipped cream or fresh mascarpone cheese, or serve them over cake.

CHESTNUT CINNAMON CANDY Substitute 1 cinnamon stick for the vanilla bean.

CHESTNUT SPICED CANDY Omit the vanilla bean. Add 1 bay leaf, 4 or 5 fresh sage leaves, and 1 teaspoon fennel or anise seed to the water with the chestnuts.

PUMPKIN CANDY Omit chestnuts. Follow the same technique using 4 cups cubed fresh pumpkin meat. Omit step 1.

SQUASH CANDY Omit chestnuts. Follow the same technique using 4 cups cubed fresh butternut squash or blue Hubbard squash meat. Omit step 1.

MARSHMALLOWS

Contrary to popular myth, marshmallows are not made from egg whites. They are made from gelatin beaten with a cooked sugar syrup. The texture of these homemade marshmallows is denser than the store-bought variety, and the flavor, more intense. People will think you're a master pastry chef as soon as they've taken their first bite.

> 3 envelopes unflavored gelatin
> 1½ cups water
> 2 cups granulated sugar
> 1 cup light corn syrup
> 1 tablespoon vanilla extract
> Vegetable oil for coating the pan
> Confectioners' sugar for coating the candy

1· Oil a 9 × 13-inch pan and set it aside.

2· In a large mixing bowl, sprinkle the gelatin over ¾ cup water. Cover the bowl and set it aside to allow the gelatin to soften until needed.

3· Combine the sugar, ¾ cup corn syrup, and the remaining ¾ cup water in a heavy medium saucepan. Place the pan over medium heat. Stir until the sugar dissolves completely and the mixture comes to a boil.

4· Clip a candy thermometer to the inside of the pan and cook the syrup without stirring until it reaches 240°F (soft ball). Remove the pan from the heat and add the remaining ¼ cup corn syrup.

5· With the mixer on high, beat the hot syrup into the large bowl containing the softened gelatin in a slow steady stream. Beat for 10 minutes, or until the mixture triples in volume and becomes very stiff. Beat in the vanilla.

6· Spread the mixture into the prepared pan. Smooth the top as much as possible using a thin, flexible spatula or a wide knife dipped in water. Set aside uncovered for 8 to 10 hours at room temperature, or until the mixture is cool and firm.

7· Dust a large cutting board with confectioners' sugar. Sift additional confectioners' sugar over the top of the marshmallow. Don't skimp. Run a small knife around the edge of the marshmallow to loosen it from the pan. Invert the pan onto the prepared cutting board. You may need to coax the marshmallow out of the pan with your fingers. It may also be a little sticky. Sift more confectioners' sugar over the marshmallow once you have unmolded it.

8· Cut the marshmallow into 3-inch squares using a sharp knife or a pizza roller. Dip the cut sides of the marshmallows in additional confectioners' sugar. Shake off the excess sugar and store the marshmallows in an airtight container at room temperature for up to 3 weeks.

VARIATIONS

ALMOND MARSHMALLOWS Add ½ teaspoon almond extract with the vanilla. Substitute 2 pounds ground toasted almonds for the confectioners' sugar used for coating the marshmallows. For advice on toasting nuts, see page 12.

COCOA MARSHMALLOWS Substitute unsweetened cocoa powder for the confectioners' sugar used to coat the marshmallows.

COCONUT MARSHMALLOWS Beat in 2 cups shredded sweetened coconut with the vanilla extract.

HALLOWEEN MARSHMALLOWS Add 5 drops orange or black food coloring with the vanilla.

LEMON MARSHMALLOWS Substitute 2 teaspoons lemon extract and 5 drops yellow food coloring for the vanilla extract.

MINTY MARSHMALLOWS Substitute 2 teaspoons mint extract and 5 drops green food coloring for the vanilla extract.

TOASTED COCONUT MARSHMALLOWS Substitute 4 cups toasted, shredded sweetened coconut for the confectioners' sugar used to coat the marshmallows. For advice on toasting coconut, see page 12.

VALENTINE'S DAY MARSHMALLOWS Add 5 drops red food coloring with the vanilla. Cut out marshmallows with heart-shaped cookie cutters.

MARSHMALLOW CUPS

A crisp chocolate shell surrounds a creamy marshmallow filling. These are mouthwatering at room temperature, unbelievable from the refrigerator—and unforgettable served from the freezer.

> 24 ounces semi-sweet chocolate, coarsely chopped, or 24 ounces semisweet chocolate chips
>
> 1 cup marshmallow cream
>
> 48 small paper candy cups, about 1½ inches in diameter

1· Melt 12 ounces of the semisweet chocolate in the top of a double boiler set over hot water. If you don't have a double boiler, simply place the chocolate in a bowl that fits snugly over a pot of hot water.

2· When the chocolate has melted completely, remove the top part of the double boiler or the bowl from the hot water. Add the remaining 12 ounces of semisweet chocolate, and stir until all of the chocolate is melted and smooth.

3· Insert a candy thermometer or chocolate thermometer into the melted chocolate. Its temperature should be 88 to 90°F. If the chocolate is too cold, place it back over the hot water until the temperature reaches 88 to 90°F. If it is too hot, let it cool until the desired temperature is reached.

4· Double the paper candy cups to make them sturdier and easier to handle. Using a 1-inch pastry brush, coat the bottom and sides of the cups to a ¼-inch thickness. Set the 24 chocolate-lined cups on a platter and place them in the refrigerator for 10 minutes. Place the remaining chocolate back over the warm water until you are ready to use it.

5· Spoon the marshmallow cream into a Ziploc bag and seal the bag, after removing as much air as possible. Using a pair of scissors, cut off one bottom corner of the bag, making a ½-inch hole. Squeeze the marshmallow cream through this hole into the bottom of the chocolate cups, using about 2 teaspoons of marshmallow cream for each cup. Alternatively, you can use a small pastry bag fitted with a ½-inch plain round tip.

6· Transfer the remaining melted chocolate to a measuring cup with a handle and spout. Pour the chocolate over the marshmallow centers, filling the cups to the top.

7· Let the marshmallow cups rest at room temperature until the chocolate is set, about 4 hours. The cooler your room's temperature, the faster the chocolate will harden. You can speed up the process by placing the cups in the refrigerator for 10 minutes, but no longer. Store the cups in layers, separated by wax paper, in an airtight container at room temperature for up to 1 week.

8· If you don't mind a dull finish, you may cool and store the marshmallow cups in the refrigerator. They are especially delicious this way and will last for up to 3 weeks. Or store them in the freezer for up to 3 months.

VARIATIONS

BUTTERSCOTCH MARSHMALLOW CUPS Substitute 24 ounces butterscotch chips for the semisweet chocolate.

MILK CHOCOLATE MARSHMALLOW CUPS Substitute 24 ounces milk chocolate for the semisweet chocolate.

WHITE CHOCOLATE MARSHMALLOW CUPS Substitute 24 ounces white chocolate for the semisweet chocolate.

The following variations work with the base recipe or with any of the preceding variations.

MARSHMALLOW BUTTERSCOTCH CUPS Reduce the amount of marshmallow cream to ½ cup. Spoon 1 teaspoon jarred butterscotch ice cream topping into the bottom of each chocolate cup before adding 1 teaspoon marshmallow cream.

MARSHMALLOW CARAMEL CUPS Reduce the amount of marshmallow cream to ½ cup. Spoon 1 teaspoon jarred caramel ice cream topping into the bottom of each chocolate cup before adding 1 teaspoon marshmallow cream.

MARSHMALLOW PEANUT CUPS Add 2 or 3 salted peanuts to the bottom of each chocolate cup before adding the marshmallow cream.

MARSHMALLOW RAISIN CUPS Add 2 or 3 raisins to the bottom of the each chocolate cup before adding the marshmallow cream.

MARSHMALLOWMAR CUPS Sprinkle 1 teaspoon crumbled graham crackers into the bottom of each chocolate cup before adding the marshmallow cream.

MARZIPAN PINECONES

Candy maven Michelle T. Miller taught me how to make these unique confections. With marzipan at the center and a shell of overlapping almond slices, these candy pinecones look amazingly like the real thing. The recipe is fun to make but takes patience and time. You will create a work of art that will look extraordinary decorating holiday desserts like a bûche de Noël.

> 7 ounces almond paste (available in the baking aisle of most supermarkets)
>
> ¼ cup marshmallow cream
>
> 2 tablespoons light corn syrup
>
> 1 cup plus 2 tablespoons confectioners' sugar
>
> 16 ounces slivered almonds
>
> ¼ cup cocoa powder

1· Combine the almond paste, marshmallow cream, and corn syrup in a large mixing bowl. Beat well by hand or with an electric mixer until thoroughly combined. Slowly add 1 cup of the confectioners' sugar and beat until a semifirm dough is formed.

2· Turn the dough onto a large cutting board or the counter, and knead the dough with the heels of your hands for a few minutes to ensure that all the ingredients are well blended and the marzipan is smooth.

3· Divide the dough into 6 pieces. Shape each piece like a small football. Working with one piece at a time, choose only the largest whole slices of almond and gently insert them halfway, one at a time, into the piece of marzipan. Start at the bottom and circle your way up, creating overlapping "shingles." Once the entire piece is covered in almond shingles, it should resemble a pinecone. Fill in any empty spaces with almond slices.

4· When all 6 pinecones are finished, use a 1-inch pastry brush to brush the pinecones with cocoa powder. Use the remaining confectioners' sugar to dust the pinecones to simulate snow.

5. Store the marzipan pinecones in one layer in an airtight container at room temperature for up to 2 weeks.

SERVING SUGGESTIONS

• These marzipan candies make a beautiful dessert table decoration.

• Use them to decorate the top of a chocolate or almond cake.

• Lean place cards against them on a small plate at a formal dinner table and allow your guests to take the pinecones home.

• Six of these pinecones in a Japanese wooden box, tied with raffia, makes a unique and delicious holiday gift.

• Drizzle with melted white or dark chocolate and let the chocolate set before brushing with cocoa and dusting with confectioners' sugar. For advice on melting chocolate, see page 11.

• Drizzle with melted caramel and let the caramel set before brushing with cocoa and dusting with confectioners' sugar.

MERINGUE KISSES

Think of these as baked candies. They are beaten egg whites with sugar that are light as air—and fat-free. Serve them with sorbet for dessert, or with a cup of tea in the afternoon.

2 large egg whites

¼ teaspoon salt

¼ teaspoon cream of tartar

1 cup superfine sugar

2 teaspoons vanilla extract

Butter or margarine to grease the cookie sheets

1· Preheat the oven to 180° F. Butter two large cookie sheets and line them with parchment paper. Set the sheets aside.

2· In a medium mixing bowl, beat the egg whites and salt with an electric mixer on high until they are foamy. Add the cream of tartar and continue to beat until soft peaks form. Beat in the sugar a few tablespoons at a time. Continue beating until you no longer feel any sugar when you rub a little of the mixture between your fingers. Add the vanilla and beat until it is well incorporated.

3· Drop by tablespoonsful onto the prepared cookie sheets. Leave a little peak at the top of each one.

4· Bake for 1½ hours. Turn off the heat, prop the oven door open, and allow the kisses to cool completely in the oven.

5· Peel the cooled kisses off the parchment and store them in airtight containers at room temperature for up to 2 weeks.

VARIATIONS

ALMOND MERINGUE KISSES Add ½ cup sliced almonds with the vanilla extract.

BUTTERSCOTCH MERINGUE KISSES Add ½ cup butterscotch chips with the vanilla extract.

CHOCOLATE CHIP MERINGUE KISSES Mix in ⅓ cup miniature chocolate chips with the vanilla extract.

CIRCUS MERINGUES Sprinkle the tops with a little colored sugar before baking.

LEMON MERINGUE KISSES Substitute 1 teaspoon lemon extract and ½ teaspoon grated fresh lemon rind for the vanilla. If desired, you may also add 2 drops yellow food coloring with the extract.

MOLASSES TAFFY

This taffy starts out black and becomes golden as you pull it. It's hard work, but worth every bite. If you like Mary Jane's, you'll love this candy.

1½ cups unsulfured molasses

1½ cups sugar

2 tablespoons butter plus additional for greasing the pan and the cookie sheet

1 tablespoon white vinegar

1· **COOKING THE TAFFY** Generously butter a 9 × 13-inch baking pan and set aside.

2· Combine the molasses, sugar, butter, and vinegar in a 3-quart heavy pan. Place the pan over medium heat. Stir until the sugar is completely dissolved and the mixture comes to a boil.

3· Clip a candy thermometer to the inside of the pan and cook, without stirring, until the mixture reaches 260°F (hard ball).

4· Pour the hot syrup into the prepared 9 × 13-inch pan and allow it to cool until the bottom of the pan feels warm, but not hot. The taffy will still be soft and slightly runny, and is now ready to be pulled.

5· **PULLING THE TAFFY** Butter a large cookie sheet (preferably nonstick) or butter a large marble slab. If you have a marble or granite counter, by all means use it. Simply clean it, then generously butter it.

6· Pour the warm candy onto the prepared work surface. Lightly butter your hands and start folding the taffy onto itself by taking the corners and bringing them up onto the middle of the taffy. Continue folding the corners back onto the center until the taffy can be gathered into a ball, about 3 minutes. The taffy is now ready to be pulled. If your hands are small, you may divide this ball of taffy into 2 or 3 pieces before you begin to pull the candy.

7· Holding the ball of taffy with both hands, pull it into a rope about 2 feet long, twisting the rope as you pull. Bring the ends of the rope together, creating a shorter, 1-foot rope. Pull this 1-foot rope of taffy to a length of 2 feet or more, twisting the rope as you pull. Bring the ends together again. Repeat this process until the taffy becomes golden and is very hard to pull, about 10 minutes.

8· Divide the pulled taffy into 4 pieces. Roll or pull each piece into a rope about ½ inch in diameter. Cut each rope into bite-sized pieces with buttered scissors.

9· Wrap the cooled taffy pieces individually in wax paper and store them all in an air-tight container at room temperature for up to 3 weeks.

VARIATIONS

GINGER MOLASSES TAFFY Add ½ teaspoon ground ginger to the pan with the other ingredients, and ½ cup finely chopped candied ginger before pouring the syrup into the buttered pan.

PEANUT MOLASSES TAFFY Add ¾ cup finely chopped salted peanuts before pouring the syrup into the buttered pan.

SPICED MOLASSES TAFFY Add ½ teaspoon ground ginger, ½ teaspoon ground cinnamon, ¼ teaspoon ground mace, and ⅛ teaspoon ground nutmeg to the pan with all the other ingredients.

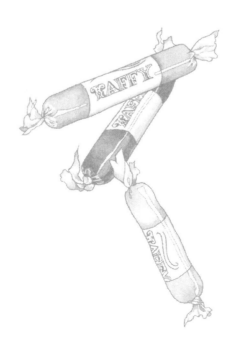

NOUGAT

Nougat is a popular candy in Italy and France. Like divinity, it is made with egg whites and sugar. The difference is that the sugar is cooked to a lower temperature in nougat, creating a softer candy. Commercially made nougat is often covered in edible rice paper. This makes for easy handling. Check the Source Guide on page 242 for this specialty item. Without it, you'll have to grease a baking pan and dust it with lots of cornstarch to prevent any sticking.

2 large egg whites
1⅓ cups light corn syrup
¾ cup sugar
⅓ cup water
2 teaspoons vanilla extract
½ cup slivered almonds
Butter or margarine for greasing the pan
Cornstarch for coating the buttered pan

1· Generously butter a 9 × 13-inch baking pan (bottom and sides) and coat the buttered pan with cornstarch. Shake out any excess cornstarch. Set the pan aside. Alternatively, line the unbuttered pan with a double layer of edible rice paper, overlapping as many sheets as necessary to cover the bottom and sides of the pan. Set the pan aside.

2· In a large mixing bowl, beat the egg whites with an electric mixer on high, until soft peaks form. Set them aside.

3· Combine the corn syrup, sugar, and water in a heavy medium saucepan. Place the pan over medium heat. Stir until the sugar is completely dissolved and the mixture comes to a boil.

4· Clip a candy thermometer to the inside of the pan and cook, without stirring, until the syrup reaches 240°F (soft ball). Do not turn off the heat.

5· Ladle 1 cup of the hot syrup into a Pyrex measuring cup with a handle and spout. Allow the remaining syrup in the pan to continue boiling.

6· Beat the egg whites on high speed for a few seconds to reincorporate any separation. Pouring the syrup in a thin stream, slowly beat it into the egg whites. Continue to beat the egg whites until the remaining syrup in the pan reaches 275°F (soft crack).

7· Slowly beat the remaining syrup, in a thin stream, into the egg white mixture. Continue beating until the mixture cools slightly, about 10 minutes. Beat in the vanilla, then fold in the nuts until they are completely incorporated.

8· Using a spatula dipped in water, spread the nougat into the prepared pan all the way to the edges.

9· If you've used butter and cornstarch, sift more cornstarch over the top of the nougat. If you've used edible rice paper, cover the top of the nougat with additional paper, overlapping as necessary to completely cover the candy. Set the pan on a cooling rack to allow the nougat to cool and firm up, about 2 hours.

10· Run a thin knife around the edges of the pan to loosen the nougat. Invert the pan and unmold the nougat onto a cutting board. Cut the nougat into 2-inch squares. If desired, dip the edges in cornstarch to prevent sticking. Store the nougat in an airtight container in layers, separated by wax paper, or wrap each piece individually in wax paper. Keep the nougat at room temperature for up to 2 weeks.

VARIATIONS

CHOCOLATE NOUGAT Add ¼ pound melted semisweet chocolate with the vanilla to the beaten egg whites. For advice on melting chocolate, see page 11.

TORRONE Reduce the amount of the corn syrup to 1 cup. Add ⅓ cup honey with the remaining corn syrup.

WHITE CHOCOLATE NOUGAT Add ¼ pound melted white chocolate with the vanilla to the beaten egg whites. For advice on melting chocolate, see page 11.

ORANGE *PÂTE DE FRUITS*

*P*âte de fruits is a French jellied fruit confection. It is not a fruit leather, but a soft candy square made by cooking fresh fruit and sugar down to a thick paste, which can take hours on end. This version uses jam instead of fresh fruit, making the process quicker and the variety of flavors seasonless.

> 2 envelopes unflavored gelatin
> ⅔ cup water
> ¾ cup granulated sugar
> 1 cup orange marmalade
> Vegetable oil for coating the pan
> Superfine sugar for coating the candy

1· Oil an 8-inch square pan. Set it aside.

2· In a small bowl, sprinkle the gelatin over ⅓ cup water. Let the gelatin soften at room temperature until needed.

3· Combine the remaining ⅓ cup water and the granulated sugar in a heavy medium saucepan. Place the pan over medium heat. Stir until the sugar dissolves and the mixture comes to a boil.

4· Add the marmalade and stir until it melts into the syrup completely. Add the softened gelatin and stir until the gelatin dissolves completely. Return the mixture to a boil and cook for 2 minutes.

5· Remove the pot from the heat and pour the syrup into the prepared 8-inch pan. Place the pan in the refrigerator until the candy is set, at least 4 hours.

6· Cover the top of the candy with superfine sugar. Use a wet knife to cut the candy into small squares. Using a narrow spatula dipped in water, carefully remove one square at a time and cover each one completely with additional superfine sugar. Store the *pâte de fruits* in layers, separated by wax paper, in an airtight container at room temperature for up to 3 weeks.

VARIATIONS

APRICOT *PÂTE DE FRUITS* Substitute 1 cup apricot jam for the orange marmalade.

BLACKBERRY *PÂTE DE FRUITS* Substitute 1 cup blackberry jam for the orange marmalade.

BLUEBERRY *PÂTE DE FRUITS* Substitute 1 cup blueberry jam for the orange marmalade.

CHERRY *PÂTE DE FRUITS* Substitute 1 cup cherry jam for the orange marmalade.

FIG *PÂTE DE FRUITS* Substitute 1 cup fig jam for the orange marmalade.

GINGER *PÂTE DE FRUITS* Substitute 1 cup ginger jam for the orange marmalade.

GRAPE *PÂTE DE FRUITS* Substitute 1 cup grape jam for the orange marmalade.

GRAPEFRUIT *PÂTE DE FRUITS* Substitute 1 cup grapefruit marmalade for the orange marmalade.

LEMON *PÂTE DE FRUITS* Substitute 1 cup lemon marmalade for the orange marmalade.

LIME *PÂTE DE FRUITS* Substitute 1 cup lime marmalade for the orange marmalade.

PEACH *PÂTE DE FRUITS* Substitute 1 cup peach jam for the orange marmalade.

PINEAPPLE *PÂTE DE FRUITS* Substitute 1 cup pineapple jam for the orange marmalade.

PLUM *PÂTE DE FRUITS* Substitute 1 cup plum jam for the orange marmalade.

QUINCE *PÂTE DE FRUITS* Substitute 1 cup quince jam for the orange marmalade.

RASPBERRY *PÂTE DE FRUITS* Substitute 1 cup raspberry jam for the orange marmalade.

RED CURRANT *PÂTE DE FRUITS* Substitute 1 cup red currant jam for the orange marmalade.

STRAWBERRY *PÂTE DE FRUITS* Substitute 1 cup strawberry jam for the orange marmalade.

ORANGETTES

Chocolate-covered orange peel is a common candy throughout France. To make it your-self, use only fresh, blemish-free oranges.

> 4 large thick-skinned oranges
>
> 6 cups water
>
> 2 cups sugar
>
> 12 ounces semisweet chocolate, coarsely chopped, or 12 ounces semisweet chocolate chips
>
> Butter or margarine for greasing the cookie sheet

1· Butter a cookie sheet and line it with wax paper. Set aside.

2· Using a sharp paring knife, cut the rinds off the oranges in the largest pieces possi-ble. Remove as much of the white pith as you can, leaving the orange rind ⅛ to ¼ inch thick.

3· Fill a heavy medium pan with 4 cups water. Add the orange rinds and bring the water to a boil. Boil for 3 minutes. Remove the rinds with a slotted spoon and discard the water.

4· Combine the sugar and remaining 2 cups water in the same pan used for blanching the orange rinds. Place the pan over medium heat. Stir until the sugar dissolves and the syrup comes to a simmer. Add the orange rinds and simmer for 10 minutes. Remove the pan from the heat and allow the rinds to cool in the syrup for at least ½ hour. You can leave the rinds in the syrup longer, up to 12 hours, giving them a more candied taste.

5· Remove the orange rinds from the syrup and place them on a cooling rack to dry, about ½ hour. Discard the syrup. When the rinds are dry (they may be a little sticky), slice them lengthwise into ¼-inch strips. Set them aside while you melt the chocolate.

6· Melt 6 ounces of the semisweet chocolate in the top of a double boiler set over hot water. If you don't have a double boiler, simply place the chocolate in a bowl that fits snugly over a pot of hot water.

7· When the chocolate has melted completely, remove the top part of the double boiler or the bowl from the hot water. Add the remaining 6 ounces of semisweet chocolate and stir until all of the chocolate is melted and smooth.

8· Insert a candy thermometer or chocolate thermometer into the melted chocolate. Its temperature should be 88 to 90°F. If the chocolate is too cold, place it back over the hot water until the temperature reaches 88 to 90°F. If it is too hot, let it cool until the desired temperature is reached.

9· Using a pair of clean tweezers, dip each slice of rind into the melted chocolate. Place the dipped rind onto the prepared cookie sheet and let the candy cool until the chocolate is set and hard, about 4 hours. The cooler your room's temperature, the faster the chocolate will harden. You can speed up the process by placing the candy in the refrigerator for 10 minutes, but no longer. Store the candy in an airtight container in layers, separated by wax paper, at room temperature for up to 2 weeks.

VARIATIONS

MILK CHOCOLATE ORANGETTES Substitute 12 ounces milk chocolate for the semisweet chocolate.

WHITE CHOCOLATE ORANGETTES Substitute 12 ounces white chocolate for the semisweet chocolate.

The following variations work with the base recipe or with the preceding chocolate variations.

CHOCOLATE GRAPEFRUIT RIND Substitute 2 to 3 medium grapefruit for the oranges.

CHOCOLATE LEMON RIND Substitute 6 to 8 lemons for the oranges.

CHOCOLATE TANGERINE RIND Substitute 6 to 8 tangerines for the oranges.

PEANUT BUTTER CUPS

Creamy peanut butter is the perfect ready-made filling for these sweet chocolate cups. I keep them in the freezer, where the chocolate gets crunchy while the peanut butter stays creamy.

> 24 ounces milk chocolate, roughly chopped, or 24 ounces milk chocolate chips
>
> 1 cup creamy peanut butter
>
> 48 small paper candy cups (about 1½ inches in diameter)

1. Melt 12 ounces of the milk chocolate in the top of a double boiler set over hot water. If you don't have a double boiler, simply place the chocolate in a bowl that fits snugly over a pot of hot water.

2. When the chocolate has melted completely, remove the top part of the double boiler or the bowl from the hot water. Add the remaining 12 ounces of milk chocolate and stir until all of the chocolate is melted and smooth.

3. Insert a candy thermometer or chocolate thermometer into the melted chocolate. Its temperature should be 86 to 88°F. If the chocolate is too cold, place it back over the hot water until the temperature reaches 86 to 88°F. If it is too hot, let it cool until the desired temperature is reached.

4. Double the paper candy cups to make them sturdier and easier to handle. Using a 1-inch pastry brush, coat the bottom and sides of the cups to a ¼-inch thickness. Set the 24 chocolate-lined cups on a platter and place them in the refrigerator for 10 minutes. Place the remaining chocolate back over the warm water until you are ready to use it.

5. Spoon the peanut butter into a Ziploc bag and seal the bag, after removing as much air as possible. Using a pair of scissors, cut off one bottom corner of the bag, making a ½-inch hole. Squeeze the peanut butter through this hole into the bottom of the chocolate cups, using about 2 teaspoons of peanut butter for each cup. Alternatively, you can use a small pastry bag fitted with a ½-inch plain round tip.

6· Transfer the remaining melted chocolate to a measuring cup with a handle and spout. Pour the chocolate over the peanut butter centers, filling the cups to the top.

7· Let the peanut butter cups rest at room temperature until the chocolate is set, about 4 hours. The cooler your room's temperature, the faster the chocolate will harden. You can speed up the process by placing the cups in the refrigerator for 10 minutes, but no longer. Store the cups in layers, separated by wax paper, in an airtight container at room temperature for up to 1 week.

8· If you don't mind a dull finish, you may cool and store the peanut butter cups in the refrigerator. They are especially delicious this way and will last for up to 3 weeks. Or store them in the freezer for up to 3 months.

VARIATIONS

SEMISWEET CHOCOLATE PEANUT BUTTER CUPS Substitute 24 ounces semisweet chocolate for the milk chocolate.

WHITE CHOCOLATE PEANUT BUTTER CUPS Substitute 24 ounces white chocolate for the milk chocolate.

The following variations work with the base recipe or with either of the preceding chocolate variations.

PEANUT BUTTER AND JELLY CUPS Reduce the amount of peanut butter to ½ cup. Spoon 1 teaspoon grape jelly into the bottom of each chocolate cup. Top the jelly with 1 teaspoon peanut butter.

PEANUT BUTTER BANANA CUPS Sprinkle 1 teaspoon crumbled banana chips onto the bottom of the chocolate cups before adding the peanut butter.

PEANUT BUTTER CRANBERRY CUPS Add 2 or 3 dried cranberries to the bottom of each chocolate cup before adding the peanut butter.

PEANUT BUTTER CRUNCH CUPS Add 2 or 3 whole salted peanuts to the bottom of each chocolate cup before adding the peanut butter.

PEANUT BUTTER FLUFF CUPS Reduce the amount of peanut butter to ½ cup. Fill a second Ziploc bag with ½ cup marshmallow cream. Fill each cup with 1 teaspoon peanut butter, then use the second bag to top the centers with 1 teaspoon marshmallow cream.

PECAN ROLL

When you stop for gas or to stretch your legs at an interstate highway service area, you're sure to find this ever-present candy. Stuckey's made an industry out of pecan rolls in the late 1960s. A little behind the times, I didn't taste my first one until recently on a road trip from Dallas to Sante Fe.

THE FONDANT FILLING

1 ¼ cups sugar

½ cup whole milk (not low-fat)

1 tablespoon light corn syrup

¼ teaspoon salt

1 teaspoon unsalted butter plus additional for greasing the pan

1 tablespoon vanilla extract

1· Generously butter a 9 × 13-inch baking pan and set it aside.

2· Combine the sugar, milk, corn syrup, and salt in a heavy tall-sided saucepan. Height is important as the milk will make the sugar syrup boil up high in the pan, and you don't want the syrup to boil over.

3· Place the pan over medium heat. Stir until the sugar dissolves completely and the mixture comes to a boil.

4· Clip a candy thermometer to the inside of the pan and cook the syrup, without stirring, until it reaches 240°F (soft ball).

5· Remove the pan from the heat and add the butter and vanilla. Immediately pour the hot syrup into the prepared 9 × 13-inch pan. Let the syrup cool undisturbed until the bottom of the pan feels lukewarm to the touch.

6· Using a heavy wooden spoon, stir the lukewarm mixture until it forms a ball. Some of this fondant may stick to the 9 × 13-inch pan. The fondant may also seize into a very hard ball that is impossible to stir. In any case, seal the ball of fondant into a 1-gallon plastic Ziploc bag, removing as much air from the bag as possible. Let the fondant rest 1 minute before continuing.

7· With the fondant sealed in the plastic bag, roll the candy with the heel of your hand, pressing down toward the counter. Continue this light kneading motion until the fondant looks smooth and creamy and feels like a firm cookie dough, about 10 minutes.

8· Remove the fondant from the bag and divide it into 4 pieces. Shape each one into a log about 1½ inches in diameter. Wrap the logs in plastic wrap and place them in the refrigerator while you make the caramel.

THE CARAMEL

  1 cup sugar
  ¾ cup light cream
  ½ cup light corn syrup
  1 teaspoon vanilla extract

1· Combine the sugar, cream, and corn syrup in a clean, heavy tall-sided pan. Again, height is important as the cream will make the sugar syrup boil up high in the pan. Place the pan over medium heat. Stir until the sugar is completely dissolved and the mixture comes to a boil.

2· Clip a candy thermometer to the inside of the pan and cook, stirring occasionally, until the syrup reaches 250°F (firm ball).

3· Remove the pan from the heat and stir in the vanilla. Pour the caramel into a shallow heatproof bowl set into a pan of hot water. The hot water will keep the caramel from getting too hard while you dip the logs into it.

THE ASSEMBLY

  3 to 4 cups roughly chopped pecans

1· While the caramel cooks, place the pecans in a shallow cake pan or soup bowl. The pecans should be at least ½ inch deep. Remove the fondant logs from the refrigerator and using tongs, dip one log into the hot caramel. Turn the log in the caramel to make sure it is completely covered with caramel. Transfer the log to the dish with the nuts and completely cover the caramel with nuts. Press as many nuts as you can against the log, since they will stick to the hot caramel. Place the finished log on a plate and set aside to cool, about 2 hours. Repeat with the remaining logs.

2· Wrap the logs in plastic wrap and store them in an airtight container at room temperature for up to 2 weeks. To serve, cut each log into ½-inch slices.

VARIATIONS

APRICOT ALMOND LOGS Knead ½ cup finely chopped dried apricots into the fondant filling before shaping it into logs. Substitute 3 to 4 cups slivered almonds for the pecans.

CASHEW LOGS Substitute 3 to 4 cups toasted, roughly chopped cashews for the pecans. For advice on toasting nuts, see page 12.

COCONUT PECAN LOGS Knead ½ cup shredded sweetened coconut into the fondant filling before shaping it into logs.

PISTACHIO CHERRY LOGS Knead ½ cup finely chopped dried cherries into the fondant filling before shaping it into logs. Substitute 3 to 4 cups shelled pistachios for the pecans.

RAISIN PEANUT LOGS Knead ½ cup golden raisins into the fondant filling before shaping it into logs. Substitute 3 to 4 cups salted peanuts for the pecans.

WALNUT LOGS Substitute 3 to 4 cups walnut pieces for the pecans.

POTATO PEANUT CANDY

These fancy little candies have only the slightest hint of potato flavor. What makes them special is the balance of sweet and salt—plus, they're very pretty. Unless you dip them in chocolate, they will dry out, so make them just a short while before you serve them.

> 1 large baking potato, about ¾ pound
>
> 5 to 6 cups confectioners' sugar
>
> 2 teaspoons vanilla extract
>
> ¼ cup (4 tablespoons) smooth peanut butter, at room temperature

1· Preheat the oven to 400°F. Bake the potato until tender, about 1 hour. Let the potato cool, then peel and mash it. You should have ¾ cup mashed plain potato.

2· Place the mashed potato in a large mixing bowl. Add 1 cup of the confectioners' sugar and the vanilla. As you mix, the potato will liquefy. Keep adding sugar ½ cup at a time until the mixture forms a soft dough.

3· Dust your counter or cutting board with confectioners' sugar. Divide the dough into three equal parts. Roll each piece of dough into a ¼-inch sheet.

4· Brush one sheet with 2 tablespoons peanut butter and top with the second potato sheet. Spread the top of the second sheet with the remaining 2 tablespoons peanut butter. Place the third sheet of potato dough on top.

5· Trim the edges to create straight lines. Cut the candy into 1-inch squares and serve immediately. Alternatively, wrap the entire block of candy in plastic wrap and store it at room temperature for up to 2 days. Cut the candy into 1-inch squares just before serving.

VARIATION

CHOCOLATE POTATO PETITS FOURS Place the potato squares on a cookie rack set over a baking sheet lined with wax paper. Pour melted chocolate over the tops and allow it to drip down, covering the candies on all sides. Set the rack in the refrigerator to allow the chocolate to set, about 15 minutes. Serve as soon as possible. You will need 12 to 16 ounces of semisweet chocolate for 48 petits fours.

PRALINES

Pralines are pecans cooked with brown sugar and cream. You can't travel anywhere in Texas without being offered one or two. Leftover pralines are wonderful crumbled and folded into vanilla ice cream, brownie batter, or even cheesecake batter.

> 2 cups cream
>
> 2 cups granulated sugar
>
> 2 cups light brown sugar
>
> 1 tablespoon vanilla extract
>
> 2 tablespoons butter, at room temperature, plus additional for greasing the cookie sheets
>
> 3 heaping cups pecan halves

1· Butter 2 large cookie sheets and line them with wax paper. Set them aside.

2· Combine the cream and both sugars in a heavy tall-sided saucepan. Height is important as the cream will cause the sugar syrup to boil up high in the pan. You don't want the sugar syrup to boil over.

3· Place the pan over medium heat. Stir until the sugars are completely dissolved and the mixture comes to a simmer.

4· Clip a candy thermometer to the inside of the pan and simmer, without stirring, until the mixture reaches 260°F (hard ball).

5· Remove the pan from the heat and add the vanilla, 2 tablespoons butter, and pecan halves. Stir only enough to coat the pecans. Too much stirring can cause the candy to crystallize and become grainy—though still quite delicious.

6· Drop tablespoonsful of the hot candy onto the prepared cookie sheets, leaving a few inches between each to allow for spreading. Let the candy sit at room temperature until it is cool and has firmed up, 2 to 3 hours.

7· Peel the pralines off the paper and store them in an airtight container at room temperature for up to 2 weeks.

VARIATIONS

COFFEE PRALINES Dissolve 1 tablespoon instant espresso powder in 1 tablespoon water. Add this liquid with the cream.

GOLDEN PRALINES Substitute 1 cup dark brown sugar for the light brown sugar.

HOT PRALINES Add ½ teaspoon or more (depending on taste) dried chili pepper flakes with the vanilla.

RUM RAISIN PRALINES Reduce the amount of pecans to 2 cups. Add 1 cup golden raisins with the remaining nuts. Substitute 1 tablespoon artificial rum flavoring for the vanilla.

WALNUT PRALINES Although a bit untraditional, you may substitute 3 cups chopped walnuts for pecans. Just don't offer them to any Texans.

PUMPKIN PECAN CANDY

These round little treats are made from canned pumpkin and unsweetened coconut chips. Look for unsweetened coconut chips or flakes in your local health food store, or consult the Source Guide on page 242.

> 2 cups sugar
>
> 2 cups unsweetened coconut chips or flakes
>
> 1¾ cups cooked pumpkin (15-ounce can)
>
> ½ teaspoon vanilla extract
>
> 3 cups chopped pecans

1· Combine the sugar, coconut, and pumpkin in a heavy medium saucepan. Place over medium heat and stir until the sugar dissolves. Continue cooking, stirring constantly, until the mixture thickens and forms into a ball, 15 to 20 minutes. Stir in the vanilla.

2· Place the cooked mixture into a bowl and set aside to cool. Cover the surface with plastic wrap or wax paper to avoid a skin forming.

3· Roll tablespoonsful of the mixture into balls between your palms. Roll the balls in the chopped pecans.

4· Store the candies in an airtight container at room temperature for up to 1 week.

VARIATIONS

PUMPKIN ALMOND CANDY Substitute 3 cups toasted chopped almonds for the pecans. For advice on toasting nuts, see page 12.

PUMPKIN PECAN RAISIN CANDY Add ½ cup golden raisins to the hot mixture before setting it aside to cool.

PUMPKIN PIE PECAN CANDY Add 1 teaspoon ground cinnamon, ¼ teaspoon ground nutmeg, and ⅛ teaspoon ground cloves before cooking the pumpkin.

SPICED PUMPKIN PECAN CANDY Add 1 tablespoon (or more to taste) ground ancho chili powder before cooking the pumpkin.

RASPBERRY CUPS

MAKES 24 CUPS

When I was in high school in New York City, my grandmother would take me to the ballet. We would always eat first in a little bistro near the Metropolitan Opera House. That's when I first tasted white chocolate—in a mousse, served with raspberry sauce. These sweet little cups combine those two flavors that I came to love.

> 24 ounces white chocolate, chopped, or
> 24 ounces white chocolate chips
>
> 1 cup raspberry jam, with or without seeds
>
> 48 small paper candy cups
> (about 1½ inches in diameter)

1· Melt 12 ounces of the white chocolate in the top of a double boiler set over hot water. If you don't have a double boiler, simply place the chocolate in a bowl that fits snugly over a pot of hot water.

2· When the chocolate has melted completely, remove the top part of the double boiler or the bowl from the hot water. Add the remaining 12 ounces of white chocolate and stir until all of the chocolate is melted and smooth.

3· Insert a candy thermometer or chocolate thermometer into the melted chocolate. Its temperature should be 86 to 88°F. If the chocolate is too cold, place it back over the hot water until the temperature reaches 86 to 88°F. If it is too hot, let it cool until the desired temperature is reached.

4· Double the paper candy cups to make them sturdier and easier to handle. Using a 1-inch pastry brush, coat the bottom and sides of the cups to a ¼-inch thickness. Set the 24 chocolate-lined cups on a platter and place them in the refrigerator for 10 minutes. Place the remaining chocolate back over the warm water until you are ready to use it.

5· Spoon the raspberry jam into a Ziploc bag and seal the bag, after removing as much air as possible. Using a pair of scissors, cut off one bottom corner of the bag, making a ½-inch hole. Squeeze the raspberry jam through this hole into the bottom of the chocolate cups, using about 2 teaspoons of raspberry jam for each cup. Alternatively, you can use a small pastry bag fitted with a ½-inch plain round tip.

6· Transfer the remaining melted chocolate to a measuring cup with a handle and spout. Pour the chocolate over the raspberry jam centers, filling the cups to the top.

7· Let the raspberry cups rest at room temperature until the chocolate is set, about 4 hours. The cooler your room's temperature, the faster the chocolate will harden. You can speed up the process by placing the cups in the refrigerator for 10 minutes, but no longer. Store the cups in layers, separated by wax paper, in an airtight container at room temperature for up to 1 week.

8· If you don't mind a dull finish, you may cool and store the raspberry cups in the refrigerator. They are especially delicious this way and will last for up to 3 weeks. Or store them in the freezer for up to 3 months.

VARIATIONS

MILK CHOCOLATE RASPBERRY CUPS Substitute 24 ounces milk chocolate for the white chocolate.

SEMISWEET CHOCOLATE RASPBERRY CUPS Substitute 24 ounces semisweet chocolate for the white chocolate.

The following variations work with the base recipe or with either of the preceding chocolate variations.

APRICOT CUPS Substitute 1 cup apricot jam for the raspberry jam. If the apricots in the jam are large, puree the jam in the food processor before placing it in the plastic bag.

BLACKBERRY CUPS Substitute 1 cup blackberry jam for the raspberry jam.

BLUEBERRY CUPS Substitute 1 cup blueberry jam for the raspberry jam.

GINGER CUPS Substitute 1 cup ginger jam for the raspberry jam. If the ginger pieces in the jam are large, puree the jam in the food processor before placing it in the plastic bag.

PEACH CUPS Substitute 1 cup peach jam for the raspberry jam. If the peaches in the jam are large, puree the jam in the food processor before placing it in the plastic bag.

STRAWBERRY CUPS Substitute 1 cup strawberry jam for the raspberry jam. If the strawberries in the jam are large, puree the jam in the food processor before placing it in the plastic bag.

SALTWATER TAFFY

Atlantic City is said to be the birthplace of saltwater taffy. Some say salt water from the Jersey shore was used to make candy. I've also heard that a storm flooded the candy shops, changing the name of taffy forever. Whatever its true origin, saltwater taffy will always be one of my favorites. This recipe calls for glycerin, which is available in any pharmacy. Glycerin helps make this taffy smooth and creamy. If you can't find glycerin, just ask the druggist, or consult the Source Guide on page 242.

2 cups sugar

1 tablespoon cornstarch

1 cup water

1½ teaspoons salt

2 teaspoons glycerin

3 tablespoons butter plus additional for greasing the pan and the cookie sheet

2 teaspoons vanilla extract

1· **COOKING THE TAFFY** Generously butter a 9 × 13-inch baking pan and set it aside.

2· Combine the sugar and cornstarch in a heavy medium saucepan and mix well. Add the water, salt, and glycerin. Stir over medium heat until the sugar is completely dissolved and the mixture comes to a boil.

3· Clip a candy thermometer to the inside of the pan and cook, without stirring, until the syrup reaches 260°F (hard ball).

4· Remove the pan from the heat and add the butter and vanilla. Stir until the butter melts and is fully incorporated. Pour the hot syrup into the prepared 9 × 13-inch pan and allow it to cool until the bottom of the pan feels warm, but not hot. The taffy will still be soft and slightly runny, and is now ready to be pulled.

5· **PULLING THE TAFFY** Butter a large cookie sheet (preferably nonstick) or butter a large marble slab. If you have a marble or granite counter, by all means use it. Simply clean it, then generously butter it.

6· Pour the warm candy onto the prepared work surface. Lightly butter your hands and start folding the taffy onto itself by taking the corners and bringing them up onto the middle of the taffy. Continue folding the corners back onto the center until the taffy can be gathered into a ball, about 3 minutes. The taffy is now ready to be pulled. If your hands are small, you may divide this ball of taffy into 2 or 3 pieces before you begin to pull the candy.

7· Holding the ball of taffy with both hands, pull it into a rope about 2 feet long, twisting the rope as you pull. Bring the ends of the rope together, creating a shorter, 1-foot rope. Pull this 1-foot rope of taffy to a length of 2 feet or more, twisting the rope as you pull. Bring the ends together again. Repeat this process until the taffy becomes glossy white and is very hard to pull, about 10 minutes.

8· Divide the pulled taffy into 4 pieces. Roll or pull each piece into a rope about ½ inch in diameter. Cut each rope into bite-sized pieces with buttered scissors.

9· Wrap the cooled taffy pieces individually in wax paper and store them all in an airtight container at room temperature for up to 3 weeks.

VARIATIONS

ALMOND SALTWATER TAFFY Substitute ½ teaspoon almond extract for the vanilla.

BANANA SALTWATER TAFFY Reduce the amount of vanilla to 1 teaspoon. Add 1 teaspoon natural or artificial banana flavoring with the butter and vanilla. Also add 2 drops yellow food coloring (optional).

BUTTER RUM SALTWATER TAFFY Substitute 1 teaspoon artificial rum flavoring and ½ teaspoon artificial butter flavoring for the vanilla.

LEMON CREAM SALTWATER TAFFY Add 1 teaspoon lemon extract with the vanilla and butter. Also add 2 drops yellow food coloring (optional).

MAPLE SALTWATER TAFFY Substitute 1 teaspoon artificial maple flavoring for the vanilla.

MINT SALTWATER TAFFY Substitute 1 teaspoon mint extract for the vanilla. Also add 2 drops green food coloring (optional).

ORANGE CREAM SALTWATER TAFFY Add 1 teaspoon orange extract with the vanilla and butter. Also add 2 drops orange food coloring (optional).

STUFFED DATES

Fruit with cheese is an elegant dessert, from pears with Parmesan to figs with mascarpone. This candy combines a ricotta cheese cannoli cream with sweet dried dates.

> 1 pound dried, pitted dates (about 4 dozen)
> 1 pound ricotta cheese (do not use fat-free)
> ½ cup sugar
> 2 teaspoons vanilla extract
> ¼ cup finely chopped pistachio nuts
> 1 teaspoon grated orange rind

1 · With a sharp knife, make a slit lengthwise through one side of each date. The dates should open up without falling into 2 pieces. Set them aside.

2 · In a medium mixing bowl, combine the ricotta, sugar, and vanilla. Beat them with an electric mixer on high speed until the mixture is smooth and creamy. Add the nuts and the orange rind. Mix until well combined.

3 · Spoon the cream filling into a Ziploc bag and seal it tight, after removing as much air as possible. Use a pair of scissors to snip off one corner of the bag, creating a ½-inch hole. Squeeze the cream filling through this hole into the split dates. Alternatively, you may use a pastry bag fitted with a plain ½-inch round tip.

4 · Cover the dates with plastic wrap and keep them refrigerated until ready to serve. The stuffed dates will keep fresh for 2 days.

VARIATIONS

BRANDIED STUFFED DATES Substitute 2 tablespoons brandy for the vanilla.

CHOCOLATE STUFFED DATES Omit the orange rind. Add 3 ounces melted semisweet chocolate to the cheese with the sugar.

STUFFED FIGS Substitute 1 pound dried black figs for the dates.

TRUFFLES

These are the most basic of all chocolate truffles. They are made from a combination of chocolate and warm cream, which is called ganache.

> 12 ounces semisweet chocolate, coarsely chopped, or 12 ounces semisweet chocolate chips
>
> ⅔ cup heavy cream
>
> 1 tablespoon unsalted butter, at room temperature
>
> 1 tablespoon vanilla extract
>
> ½ cup unsweetened cocoa, for coating

1· Place the chocolate in a medium mixing bowl. Set aside.

2· Warm the cream in a small saucepan over low heat. As soon as you start to see bubbles around the edges of the pan, turn off the heat and pour the warm cream over the chopped chocolate. Stir until the chocolate melts and the mixture is completely smooth. Add the butter and stir until it is completely incorporated. Stir in the vanilla.

3· Place the mixture in the refrigerator for 1 hour, or until it is firm enough to shape into balls.

4· Scoop out a heaping teaspoonful of the chocolate mixture and roll it into a ball between your palms. Roll the ball in cocoa until it is completely covered. Roll it lightly in your palms again to make sure the cocoa sticks, then reroll the truffle in the cocoa. Repeat with the remaining chocolate mixture. If the mixture gets too soft to hold its shape, place it back in the refrigerator for 10 minutes, or until it can be handled easily.

5· Store the truffles in layers, separated by wax paper, in an airtight container in the refrigerator for up to 2 weeks. However, they are best served at room temperature.

VARIATIONS WITH CHOCOLATE

DOUBLE SEMISWEET CHOCOLATE TRUFFLES Dip the shaped truffles into melted semisweet chocolate instead of rolling them in cocoa. For advice on melting chocolate, see page 11. You will need about 16 ounces of melted semisweet chocolate for 24 truffles.

MILK CHOCOLATE TRUFFLES Dip the shaped truffles into melted milk chocolate instead of rolling them in cocoa. For more advice on melting chocolate, see page 11. You will need about 16 ounces of melted milk chocolate for 24 truffles.

WHITE TRUFFLES Dip the shaped truffles into melted white chocolate instead of rolling them in cocoa powder. For advice on melting chocolate, see page 11. You will need about 16 ounces of melted white chocolate for 24 truffles.

The following variations work with the base recipe or with any of the preceding dipped chocolate variations.

ALMOND TRUFFLES Add 3 tablespoons almond liqueur (such as amaretto) with the butter. If desired, you may also roll the truffles in ½ cup finely chopped almonds instead of cocoa powder, or push a whole toasted almond inside the rounded truffle before rolling it in the cocoa.

CHAMPAGNE TRUFFLES Add 3 tablespoons champagne with the butter.

CHILI TRUFFLES Add 1 tablespoon ground red chili powder to the cocoa powder and combine them well before rolling the truffles in the mixture.

HONEY TRUFFLES Dissolve 2 tablespoons honey into the cream before adding the cream to the chocolate.

IRISH TRUFFLES Add 3 tablespoons whiskey with the butter.

ORANGE TRUFFLES Add 3 tablespoons orange liqueur (such as Grand Marnier) and 1 teaspoon finely grated orange rind with the butter.

RASPBERRY TRUFFLES Add 3 tablespoons raspberry liqueur (such as Chambord) with the butter.

TURKISH DELIGHT

The soft texture of this chewy candy comes from the cornstarch. The dried fruits and nuts give it the traditional flavor. Be untraditional: try the variations and then start to come up with your own.

> ¾ cup granulated sugar
>
> 1⅔ cups water
>
> ⅛ teaspoon cream of tartar
>
> 2¼ cups confectioners' sugar, plus additional for coating
>
> ½ cup cornstarch
>
> ½ teaspoon almond extract
>
> ½ cup slivered almonds, toasted (see page 12)
>
> Vegetable oil for greasing the pan

1· Line a 9 × 5-inch loaf pan with wax paper, overhanging the edges by at least 2 inches. Lightly oil the paper and set the pan aside.

2· Combine the granulated sugar, ⅔ cup water, and cream of tartar in a heavy small saucepan, set over medium heat. Stir until the sugar is completely dissolved and the mixture comes to a boil.

3· Clip a candy thermometer to the inside of the pan and cook without stirring until the syrup reaches 260°F (hard ball). Turn off the heat and cover the pan to keep the syrup warm.

4· Combine the remaining 1 cup water with 2 cups confectioners' sugar and the corn-starch in a heavy medium saucepan. Set the pan over medium heat. Stir until the sugar and cornstarch completely dissolve and the mixture comes to a boil. It will quickly become a thick paste. Immediately add the warm sugar syrup and stir until the mixture is creamy white and smooth. Return the mixture to a boil and cook for 5 minutes, stirring constantly. Remove from the heat.

5· Add the almond extract and the almonds all at once, and mix until thoroughly combined. Spread the mixture into the prepared loaf pan. Let the candy rest at room temperature overnight or until it is firm, at least 6 to 8 hours.

6· Remove the candy from the pan by lifting the wax paper. Sprinkle the top of the candy with the remaining ¼ cup confectioners' sugar. Cut the candy into bite-sized pieces and roll each piece in additional confectioners' sugar to keep them from sticking together.

7· Store the sugared pieces in an airtight container, in layers separated by wax paper, at room temperature for up to 2 weeks.

VARIATIONS

APRICOT TURKISH DELIGHT Substitute ½ teaspoon vanilla extract for the almond extract and ½ cup finely chopped dried apricots for the almonds.

BANANA ALMOND TURKISH DELIGHT Substitute 1 teaspoon natural or artificial banana flavoring for the almond extract.

LEMON TURKISH DELIGHT Substitute ½ teaspoon lemon extract for the almond extract. Omit the nuts.

MINT TURKISH DELIGHT Substitute 1 teaspoon mint extract or ¼ teaspoon peppermint oil for the almond extract. Omit the nuts.

PISTACHIO ORANGE TURKISH DELIGHT Substitute 2 teaspoons orange-flower water for the almond extract and ½ cup whole shelled pistachio nuts for the almonds. See the Source Guide on page 242 for orange-flower water.

RED HOT TURKISH DELIGHT Omit the almond extract and almonds. Instead, add 1 teaspoon crushed red chili flakes and ½ cup pecan pieces.

ROSE TURKISH DELIGHT Substitute 2 teaspoons rose water for the almond extract. See the Source Guide on page 242 for rose water.

TURKISH TAFFY

Turkey (neither the country nor the bird) has nothing to do with Turkish taffy. I grew up eating Bonomo's Turkish Taffy in bars that we froze, then cracked on the table. My recipe for Turkish taffy does not require pulling. The hot taffy is poured into a large flat pan to cool, then cut with scissors into squares—or frozen and cracked into pieces.

1 large egg white
2½ cups sugar
½ cup water
¼ teaspoon cream of tartar
1 cup orange marmalade
5 drops orange food coloring (optional)
Butter or margarine for greasing the pan

1· Butter an 11 × 17-inch jelly-roll pan or cookie sheet with high edges. Line the pan with wax paper and butter the paper. Set the pan aside.

2· In a large mixing bowl, beat the egg white with an electric mixer on high until soft peaks form. Set the beaten white aside, while you prepare the sugar syrup.

3· Combine the sugar, water, and cream of tartar in a large heavy pan. Place the pan over medium heat. Stir until the sugar is completely dissolved and the mixture comes to a boil.

4· Clip a candy thermometer to the inside of the pan and cook without stirring until the syrup reaches 260°F (hard ball). While the syrup is boiling, wash any sugar crystals down from the sides of the pans with a wet pastry brush.

5· Add the marmalade and food coloring, if using. Stir until the marmalade completely melts into the syrup. Bring the syrup back to a boil point until it reaches 260°F again. Don't worry about sugar crystals during this second boiling. Turn off the heat.

6· Refresh the egg white with a quick beating—10 seconds on high is usually enough. Continue beating on high while pouring the hot syrup into the beaten egg white in a slow, steady stream. Allow the mixer to run until the bowl feels warm but not hot, 10 to 15 minutes. The mixture will be very stiff.

7· Using a long, narrow spatula dipped in water, spread the taffy onto the prepared pan, all the way to the edges. Place the pan in the freezer to let the taffy set up, about 1 hour. When the candy is cold and firm, use your hands to crack it into irregular pieces about the size of candy bars. Alternatively, allow the taffy to soften, then cut it into 4-inch squares using buttered scissors.

8· Wrap each piece of taffy in wax paper and store them all in an airtight container at room temperature for up to 1 week, or in the refrigerator for up to 1 month, or in the freezer for up to 3 months. This candy tastes best if you wait to eat it at least 24 hours after it is made.

VARIATIONS

APRICOT TURKISH TAFFY Substitute 1 cup apricot jam for the orange marmalade. Add ¾ cup roughly chopped pistachio nuts (optional) to the mixer while the taffy is beating.

CHERRY TURKISH TAFFY Substitute 1 cup cherry jam for the orange marmalade and 5 drops red food coloring for the orange food coloring.

FIG TURKISH TAFFY Omit the orange food coloring. Substitute 1 cup fig jam for the orange marmalade. Add ¾ cup chopped almonds (optional) to the mixture while the taffy is beating.

GRAPE TURKISH TAFFY Omit the orange food coloring. Substitute 1 cup grape jam or jelly for the orange marmalade.

LIME TURKISH TAFFY Substitute 1 cup lime marmalade for the orange marmalade and 5 drops green food coloring for the orange food coloring.

PEACH TURKISH TAFFY Substitute 1 cup peach jam for the orange marmalade and 5 drops yellow food coloring for the orange food coloring.

RASPBERRY TURKISH TAFFY Substitute 1 cup raspberry jam for the orange marmalade and 5 drops red food coloring for the orange food coloring.

STRAWBERRY TURKISH TAFFY Substitute 1 cup strawberry jam for the orange marmalade and 5 drops red food coloring for the orange food coloring.

TURTLES

Every holiday my Dad would bring home boxes of candy turtles he'd gotten from the office. No candy book would be complete without them. Homemade caramels would make these very special. But you can buy individually wrapped caramels at the store and melt them with a little cream to make them taste like homemade.

½ pound caramel (about 30 small store-bought caramels)

2 tablespoons heavy cream

120 large pecan halves (about ¾ pound)

8 ounces semisweet chocolate, coarsely chopped, *or* 8 ounces semisweet chocolate chips

Butter or margarine for greasing the cookie sheet

1· Butter a large cookie sheet and line it with wax paper. Set aside.

2· Place the caramels and cream in a heavy small saucepan over low heat. Stir constantly until the caramel is melted. Remove the pan from the heat and set aside.

3· Place 5 pecan halves on the cookie sheet in a grouping to resemble a turtle's legs and head. Repeat with the remaining pecans until you have made 24 groupings.

4· Using the back of a spoon, spread 1 to 2 tablespoons of caramel over the center of each grouping of nuts. The caramel will become the turtle's shell, so you want to make sure that you leave the ends of the nuts (the head and feet) exposed. Let the caramel firm up while you melt the chocolate.

5· Melt 4 ounces of the semisweet chocolate in the top of a double boiler set over hot water. If you don't have a double boiler, simply place the chocolate in a bowl that fits snugly over a pot of hot water.

6· When the chocolate has melted completely, remove the top part of the double boiler or the bowl from the hot water. Add the remaining 4 ounces of semisweet chocolate and stir until all of the chocolate is melted and smooth.

7· Insert a candy thermometer or chocolate thermometer into the melted chocolate. Its temperature should be 88 to 90°F. If the chocolate is too cold, place it back over the hot water until the temperature reaches 88 to 90°F. If it is too hot, let it cool until the desired temperature is reached.

8· Using the back of a spoon, spread 1 to 2 tablespoons of the chocolate over the caramel to cover it completely. Remember to leave the tips of the nuts exposed. If desired, use a toothpick to draw lines in the chocolate to represent a turtle's shell. When completely set (about 4 hours at room temperature), peel the turtles off the wax paper and store them in layers, separated by wax paper, in an airtight container at room temperature for up to 1 month.

VARIATIONS

MILK CHOCOLATE TURTLES Substitute 8 ounces milk chocolate for the semisweet chocolate.

WHITE CHOCOLATE TURTLES Substitute 8 ounces white chocolate for the semisweet chocolate.

The following variations work with the base recipe or with either of the preceding chocolate variations.

ALMOND TURTLES Substitute 120 whole almonds for the pecans.

BRAZIL NUT TURTLES Substitute 120 Brazil nuts for the pecans.

CASHEW TURTLES Substitute 120 large toasted cashews for the pecans.

WALNUT TURTLES Substitute 120 walnut halves for the pecans.

VANILLA FUDGE

MAKES ABOUT 2 POUNDS

This soft fudge reminds me of vanilla cake icing. Keep it in the refrigerator and serve it cold.

> 4 cups sugar
>
> 1 cup milk
>
> ¼ cup light corn syrup
>
> ¼ teaspoon salt
>
> 4 tablespoons unsalted butter plus
>   additional for greasing the pan
>
> 1 tablespoon vanilla extract

1· Line a 10-inch square pan with wax paper, overlapping the sides by at least 2 inches. Butter the paper and set the pan aside.

2· Combine the sugar, milk, corn syrup, and salt in a heavy tall-sided saucepan. Height is important because the milk will cause the sugar syrup to boil high in the pan, and you don't want the syrup to boil over.

3· Place the pan over medium heat. Stir until the sugar is completely dissolved and the mixture comes to a boil.

4· Clip a candy thermometer to the inside of the pan and cook, without stirring, until it reaches 240°F (soft ball).

5· Remove the pan from the heat and add the butter without stirring. Allow the mixture to cool undisturbed until the thermometer reads 110°F.

6· Add the vanilla and stir vigorously with a wooden spoon until the mixture loses its gloss and thickens to the consistency of cake icing. Using a buttered spatula, spread the mixture into the prepared pan and place it in the refrigerator to cool for at least 8 hours.

7· Grab the edges of the wax paper and pull the candy out of the pan. Using a sharp knife, cut the fudge into bite-sized pieces. Store them in layers, separated by wax paper, in the refrigerator for up to 1 week.

VARIATIONS

WHITE CHOCOLATE FUDGE Add ½ pound chopped white chocolate to the pan with the milk, sugar, and corn syrup.

WHITE MINT FUDGE Substitute 1 teaspoon mint extract for the vanilla extract. If desired, you may also stir in 1 cup crushed peppermint candies with the mint extract.

WHITE NUT FUDGE Add 1 cup chopped pecans or walnuts with the vanilla.

VANILLA LOWER-FAT FUDGE

MAKES ABOUT 2 POUNDS

Not all fudge is chocolate. And not all fudge is loaded with fat. Low-fat sweetened condensed milk makes this fudge lower in fat than fudge made with cream or half-and-half—which can take away some of the guilt.

4 cups sugar

One 14-ounce can low-fat sweetened condensed milk

1 cup water

2 tablespoons light corn syrup

½ teaspoon salt

2 tablespoons vanilla extract

Butter or margarine for greasing the pan

1· Line a 10-inch square pan with wax paper, overlapping the sides by at least 2 inches. Butter the paper and set the pan aside.

2· Combine the sugar, condensed milk, water, corn syrup, and salt in a heavy tall-sided pan. Height is important because the milk will cause the sugar syrup to boil high in the pan, and you don't want the syrup to boil over.

3· Place the pan over medium heat. Stir until the sugar is completely dissolved and the mixture comes to a boil.

4· Clip a candy thermometer to the inside of the pan and cook, without stirring, until it reaches 240°F (soft ball).

5· Remove the pan from the heat and allow the mixture to cool undisturbed until the thermometer reads 110°F.

6· Add the vanilla and stir vigorously with a wooden spoon until the mixture loses its gloss and thickens to the consistency of cake icing. Using a buttered spatula, spread the mixture into the prepared pan and place it in the refrigerator to cool for at least 8 hours.

7. Grab the edges of the wax paper and pull the candy out of the pan. Using a sharp knife, cut the fudge into bite-sized pieces. Store them in layers, separated by wax paper, in the refrigerator for up to 1 week.

VARIATIONS

EIGHTEEN-CARAT GOLD FUDGE Reduce the amount of sugar to 2 cups. Add 2 cups dark brown sugar with the remaining 2 cups white sugar.

FOURTEEN-CARAT GOLD FUDGE Reduce the amount of sugar to 2 cups. Add 2 cups light brown sugar with the remaining 2 cups white sugar.

GOLDEN BLUEBERRY FUDGE Add 1 cup whole dried blueberries with the vanilla.

GOLDEN HAWAIIAN FUDGE Add ¾ cup roughly chopped macadamia nuts and ¼ cup roughly chopped dried pineapple with the vanilla.

GOLDEN PISTACHIO FUDGE Add 1 cup shelled pistachio nuts with the vanilla.

TWENTY-FOUR–CARAT GOLD FUDGE Cover the finished fudge with edible gold leaf (see Source Guide, page 242).

WHITE CHOCOLATE TRUFFLES

With only four ingredients, and no candy thermometer necessary, white chocolate truffles are the easiest truffles to make. To keep them pure white, I use artificially flavored clear vanilla. Although I usually prefer real vanilla, the taste of clear vanilla is perfectly fine for these truffles. Check the Source Guide on page 242 if you can't find clear vanilla at your grocery store.

> 16 ounces white chocolate, coarsely chopped, or 16 ounces white chocolate chips
>
> ½ cup heavy cream
>
> 1 teaspoon clear vanilla (see above) or vanilla extract
>
> Confectioners' sugar for coating

1· Place the chocolate in a medium bowl and set aside.

2· Heat the cream in a small heavy saucepan over low heat until small bubbles appear around the edge of the pan and the cream begins to give off steam. Immediately pour the hot cream over the chocolate and stir until the chocolate is melted and the mixture is smooth. Add the vanilla and stir until it is completely incorporated.

3· Place the mixture in the refrigerator for 1 hour, or until it is firm enough to shape into balls.

4· Scoop out a heaping teaspoonful of the chocolate mixture and roll it into a ball between your palms. Roll the ball in confectioners' sugar until it is completely covered. Repeat with the remaining chocolate mixture. If the mixture gets too soft to hold its shape, place it back in the refrigerator for 10 minutes, or until it can be handled easily.

5· Store the truffles in layers, separated by wax paper, in an airtight container in the refrigerator for up to 2 weeks. However, they are best served at room temperature.

VARIATIONS WITH CHOCOLATE

DOUBLE WHITE TRUFFLES Dip the shaped truffles into melted white chocolate instead of rolling them in confectioners' sugar. For advice on melting chocolate, see page 11. You will need about 20 ounces of melted white chocolate for 30 truffles.

SEMISWEET WHITE TRUFFLES Dip shaped truffles into melted semisweet chocolate instead of rolling them in confectioners' sugar. For advice on melting chocolate, see page 11. You will need about 20 ounces of melted semisweet chocolate for 30 truffles.

The following variations work with the base recipe or with either of the preceding dipped chocolate variations.

BLACK-AND-WHITE TRUFFLES Substitute cocoa powder for the confectioners' sugar used to coat the truffles.

WHITE ALMOND TRUFFLES Substitute 2 tablespoons amaretto liqueur or ½ teaspoon almond extract for the vanilla. If desired, you may also roll the truffles in ½ cup finely chopped almonds instead of confectioners' sugar.

WHITE GINGER TRUFFLES Add 1 tablespoon finely chopped candied ginger with the vanilla.

WHITE ORANGE TRUFFLES Substitute 2 tablespoons Grand Marnier for the vanilla. If desired, you may also add 2 tablespoons finely grated orange rind.

WHITE RASPBERRY TRUFFLES Substitute 2 tablespoons raspberry liqueur (such as Chambord) for the vanilla.

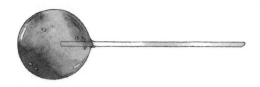

HARD *and* CRUNCHY
C a n d y

IF THERE'S ONE HARD CANDY that I love to make, eat, and give as gifts, it's lollipops. With my extensive collection of molds, I can make them for any occasion. Clear and glistening, hanging from my Christmas tree and filling baskets, boxes, and bags, they make the holidays colorful and sweet. But I've also shown up at Fourth of July barbecues with buckets of lollipops in red, white, and blue, handed out dozens of green ones to friends on St. Patrick's Day, and I make a dozen red-heart lollipops for someone very special every year. Doris Day cured her blues with a bubble bath, champagne, and truffles; I'm sure lollipops would have worked just as well.

There's more to hard candy than lollipops. Toffees, peanut brittle, lemon drops, butterscotch, and caramel corn are all waiting for you in the pages ahead.

Be careful. The recipes in this chapter require you to bring sugar to the highest temperatures in this book. It's only when sugar reaches 300°F that it becomes what candy makers call *hard crack*. At this point the sugar will cool into glistening hard candy, but it can also cause a nasty burn before it cools. So work with a bowl of ice water nearby and keep any children out of the kitchen until you're ready to serve your treats.

ALMOND CRUNCH

This recipe will work best if you use the heaviest saucepan you own. Thick metals (especially copper) conduct heat evenly and allow you to caramelize the sugar without hot spots, thereby creating a uniform coating for the nuts. There's no need for a candy thermometer because you are going to "burn" the sugar. As soon as it turns amber and smells like caramel, you'll know it's done. But you'll have to work fast, because sugar at that high temperature continues to cook even after you remove it from the heat.

> 2 cups sugar
>
> 1 cup hot water
>
> ¼ teaspoon salt
>
> 2½ cups toasted whole almonds (see page 12)
>
> Butter or margarine for greasing the cookie sheet

1· Butter a large cookie sheet (preferably nonstick) and set it aside. Alternatively, you can butter a large marble slab.

2· Combine the sugar, water, and salt in a heavy medium saucepan. Stir over medium heat until the sugar dissolves completely. Raise the heat to high and bring the syrup to a boil without stirring. Wash down any sugar crystals that form on the sides of the pan with a wet pastry brush.

3· Continue to cook the syrup without stirring until it turns a golden amber color, about 10 minutes.

4· Immediately remove the pan from the heat and add the almonds all at once. Stir the syrup with a wooden spoon until all the almonds are completely coated.

5· Pour the candy out onto the prepared sheet and use a narrow buttered spatula to spread the nuts as thinly as possible. Alternatively, use two buttered forks to pull the candy into small, thin clumps.

6· Allow the almond crunch to cool completely, about 1 hour.

7. Using your hands, break the candy into 2-inch to 3-inch irregular pieces. Store the candy in an airtight container at room temperature for up to 2 months.

VARIATIONS

HAZELNUT CRUNCH Substitute 2½ cups whole toasted hazelnuts for the almonds. For advice on toasting nuts, see page 12.

MARDI GRAS ALMOND CRUNCH Sprinkle colorful nonpareils over the candy as soon as you pour it out of the pan. The nonpareils will stick and give the candy a festive look.

PINE NUT CRUNCH Substitute 2½ cups lightly toasted pine nuts for the almonds. For advice on toasting nuts, see page 12.

PISTACHIO CRUNCH Substitute 2½ cups lightly toasted pistachio nuts for the almonds. For advice on toasting nuts, see page 12.

WALNUT CRUNCH Substitute 2½ cups lightly toasted walnut halves for the almonds. For advice on toasting nuts, see page 12.

APRICOT JEWELS

These soft and chewy dried apricots are covered with a thin, crisp candy shell. Turkish apricots have the best consistency for this recipe and are usually thicker than other dried apricots. They're also easier to dip into the sugar syrup. The candy coating in this recipe works well with many other fruits, as you'll see in the Variations. Note that candy-coated fresh fruit must be eaten within 24 hours as the candy coating will begin to soften and melt. This particular coating requires no candy thermometer. You'll know it's ready by its amber color and rich caramel aroma.

> 36 dried Turkish apricots
> 5 cups sugar
> 1 cup water
> ½ cup corn syrup
> Butter or margarine for greasing the cookie
>   sheet

1· Butter a large cookie sheet and line it with parchment paper. Set it aside.

2· Insert a bamboo skewer into the flat edge of each apricot to create an apricot lollipop. Place the prepared apricots on the wax paper while you cook the candy coating.

3· Combine the sugar, water, and corn syrup in a heavy medium saucepan and place over medium heat. Stir until the sugar dissolves completely. Bring the syrup to a boil without stirring, washing down any sugar crystals that form on the sides of the pan with a wet pastry brush. Continue to cook the syrup without stirring until it turns a light amber. Immediately remove the pan from the heat.

4· Dip each apricot into the syrup up to the skewer. Gently twirl the skewer to remove as much excess syrup as possible, leaving a thin candy coating. If a thicker candy coating is desired, simply tap off the excess syrup on the pan's edge. Transfer the dipped apricot to the prepared pan. If an apricot falls off the skewer into the syrup, use two forks to get it out. Tap the apricot on the edge of the pan to remove any excess coating and transfer it to the prepared cookie sheet.

5· The syrup will continue to cook and darken as you dip the apricots, so no matter how fast you work, the first apricots you dip will have a light golden coating and the last few will have a darker coating and a deeper taste. If you prefer a more consistent color and taste, immediately pour the hot syrup into another pan. This cools the syrup faster and slows the cooking process. But it also causes the syrup to thicken faster, making it more difficult to dip the last few apricots.

6· When all the apricots are dipped, gently pull the skewers from the fruit and allow the apricot jewels to cool and the coating to harden. Store the candy in an airtight container at room temperature for up to 1 week.

VARIATIONS

DRIED DATE JEWELS Substitute 30 to 36 dried pitted dates for the apricots.

DRIED PEAR JEWELS Substitute 24 to 30 dried pears for the apricots.

DRIED PRUNE JEWELS Substitute 30 to 36 dried pitted prunes for the apricots.

FRESH APPLE JEWELS Substitute 24 to 30 small fresh apple wedges for the apricots. Do not twirl the apples to remove any excess coating or the fruit will fall into the syrup every time. Gently tap the skewer on the edge of the pan, then transfer the fruit to the prepared cookie sheet.

FRESH BANANA JEWELS Substitute 24 to 30 1-inch banana slices for the apricots. Do not twirl the fruit to remove any excess coating or the fruit will fall into the syrup every time. Gently tap the skewer on the edge of the pan, then transfer the fruit to the prepared cookie sheet.

FRESH GRAPE JEWELS Substitute several small clusters of grapes for the apricots. If the vine has a long enough "handle," you can dip it as is without burning your fingers. Kitchen tongs can also be used to hold the cluster of grapes before dipping them into the hot syrup. Both the grapes and their vines will become candy-coated. The candied grapes can be eaten right off the candied vines once they are cooled.

FRESH ORANGE JEWELS Substitute 36 whole orange sections for the apricots. Do not twirl the fruit to remove any excess coating or the sections will fall into the syrup every time. Gently tap the skewer on the edge of the pan, then transfer the fruit to the prepared cookie sheet.

FRESH STRAWBERRY JEWELS Substitute 36 large fresh strawberries for the apricots. Do not twirl the fruit to remove any excess coating or the berries will fall into the syrup every time. Gently tap the skewer on the edge of the pan, then transfer the fruit to the prepared cookie sheet.

BURNT SUGAR LOLLIPOPS

*B*urnt sugar is a southern term for caramelized sugar. It can be lightly golden or dark amber, depending on how far you burn it. Burnt sugar is very fragile. Keep these lollipops small and you'll have fewer broken ones.

> 2 cups sugar
> ½ cup corn syrup
> ¼ cup water
> ¼ teaspoon cream of tartar
> 10 to 12 lollipop sticks
> Vegetable oil for the cookie sheet and
>   parchment

1· Oil a large cookie sheet and cover it with parchment paper. Oil the parchment and set the sheet aside.

2· Combine the sugar, corn syrup, water, and cream of tartar in a heavy medium saucepan. Set over medium heat and stir until the sugar is completely dissolved. Bring the syrup to a boil without stirring, washing down any sugar crystals that form on the sides of the pan with a wet pastry brush. Continue to cook the syrup without stirring until it turns a light amber.

3· Remove the pan from the heat and allow the bubbles to subside. Using half the syrup, pour 2-inch circles onto the prepared parchment, leaving at least 4 inches between each. Set the hot pan aside while you place the lollipops sticks—but work fast, as the remaining syrup will cool quickly, becoming too thick to pour.

4· Create the lollipops by laying the sticks onto the sheet so that the tip of each stick lies at the center of its own circle.

5· Now pour the remaining syrup over the circles, thereby "locking" the sticks into the lollipop. During this second pouring, some of the syrup may spread out over the edges of the first circle, creating slightly larger lollipops.

6· Allow the lollipops to cool completely before peeling them off the parchment.

7· Wrap the lollipops individually in wax paper or in small plastic lollipop bags. Store the candies at room temperature for up to 2 months.

VARIATIONS

CARDAMOM BURNT SUGAR LOLLIPOPS Add 10 cardamom pods to the pan with the sugar. Remove the pods before pouring the syrup.

CINNAMON BURNT SUGAR LOLLIPOPS Add one 4-inch cinnamon stick to the pan with the sugar. Remove the cinnamon stick before pouring the syrup.

GINGER BURNT SUGAR LOLLIPOPS Add 6 thick slices fresh ginger to the pan with the sugar. Remove the ginger before pouring the syrup.

BUTTERSCOTCH DROPS

Butterscotch candy gets its unmistakable flavor from butter and just a hint of vinegar. These drops can be made by pouring the hot syrup out as small disks on a flat surface, or by pouring the hot syrup into candy molds. For my money, candy molds are a good investment because you can create uniform candies time after time. To purchase candy molds, check your local kitchenware store or consult the Source Guide on page 242.

> 2 cups sugar
>
> ⅓ cup light corn syrup
>
> ½ cup unsalted butter, at room temperature, plus additional for greasing the molds or cookie sheet
>
> 3 tablespoons water
>
> 1 tablespoon white vinegar
>
> ⅛ teaspoon cream of tartar
>
> 4 drops yellow food coloring (optional)

1· Lightly butter hard-candy molds and set them aside. Alternatively, butter a large cookie sheet and line it with parchment paper. Butter the parchment and set the sheet aside.

2· Combine the sugar, corn syrup, butter, water, vinegar, and cream of tartar in a large heavy saucepan. Set over medium heat and stir until the sugar is completely dissolved and the syrup comes to a boil.

3· Clip a candy thermometer to the inside of the pan and cook until the mixture reaches 300°F (hard crack). If the syrup boils high in the pan, adjust the heat or stir gently to prevent it from spilling over. Remove the pan from the heat and allow the bubbling to subside. Stir in the food coloring.

4· Pour the hot syrup into the prepared candy molds, following the manufacturer's instructions. Alternatively, pour teaspoonsful of the hot syrup onto the prepared cookie sheet, spacing them ½ inch apart. Transferring the hot syrup to a Pyrex measuring cup with a handle and a spout often makes shaping the candies much easier.

5· When the candies are completely cool, pop them out of the molds or peel them off the parchment. Store the candies in an airtight container at room temperature for up to 2 months.

VARIATIONS

BUTTERSCOTCH CRACK-UP Pour the hot syrup into a well-buttered 9 × 13-inch pan. When cold, remove the butterscotch block from the pan and use your hands to break it into irregular pieces.

BUTTERSCOTCH RUM DROPS Add 1 teaspoon artificial rum flavoring to the cooked syrup before pouring it into the prepared molds or onto the prepared parchment paper.

GOLDEN BUTTERSCOTCH DROPS Reduce the amount of sugar to 1 cup. Add 1 cup light brown sugar with the corn syrup.

MOLASSES BUTTERSCOTCH DROPS Substitute ⅓ cup molasses for the corn syrup.

VANILLA BUTTERSCOTCH DROPS Add 1 tablespoon vanilla extract to the cooked syrup before pouring it into the prepared molds or onto the prepared parchment.

CANDY APPLES

When I was a kid, neighbors would give these out when my friends and I went trick-or-treating. Okay, today you can't do that, but you can make these for your Halloween party, or for your own kids. Many people use Red Delicious or other sweet apples, but I prefer crisp, tart apples: Macoun, McIntosh, or Granny Smith.

> 12 medium apples
> 12 long wooden lollipop sticks or chopsticks
> 3 cups sugar
> 1½ cups light corn syrup
> ¾ cup water
> 15 drops red food coloring
> Butter or margarine for greasing the cookie sheet

1· Butter a cookie sheet and line it with parchment paper. Butter the parchment and set the sheet aside.

2· Wash and thoroughly dry the apples. Remove the stems and turn the apples upside down. Since the tops are usually larger and flatter, the apples should stay upright. Insert a wooden stick into the base of each apple, pushing about two-thirds of the way through. Set the prepared apples aside.

3· Combine the sugar, corn syrup, and water in a heavy medium saucepan. Stir over low heat until the sugar is completely dissolved and the syrup comes to a boil.

4· Clip a candy thermometer to the inside of the pan and cook the syrup, without stirring, until it reaches 310°F (a little beyond hard crack). Remove the pan from the heat and stir in the food coloring. Let the syrup sit until it stops bubbling.

5· Tilt the pan to create a deep pool of sugar syrup. Dip one apple into the syrup, turning it as necessary to cover it completely. Allow any excess syrup to drip back into the pan, then place the apple on the prepared cookie sheet. Repeat with the remaining apples. Allow the coated apples to cool completely, about 1 hour. Peel the apples off the parchment and serve as soon as possible.

6· The cooled apples can be also kept loosely wrapped in wax paper at room temperature for up to 2 days.

VARIATIONS

ALMOND CANDY APPLES Add ¼ teaspoon almond extract with the food coloring.

CINNAMON CANDY APPLES Add ½ cup cinnamon red hot candies with the sugar and corn syrup.

COCONUT CANDY APPLES Before making the syrup, fill a small baking pan with sweetened, shredded coconut, at least ½ inch deep. After dipping one apple in the syrup, allow the excess to drip back into the pan, then immediately stand it up on the coconut. The coconut will stick to the candy coating and create a flat bottom. Roll the apple in the coconut to make sure that all the candy is covered. Place the apple on the parchment paper and allow it to cool. Repeat with remaining apples, adding more coconut to the pan as needed.

DOUBLE CANDY APPLES Add 1 teaspoon artificial apple candy flavoring to the syrup with the food coloring. For apple candy flavoring, look in the baking aisle of your grocery store or consult the Source Guide on page 242.

GREEN CANDY APPLES Use Granny Smith apples. Omit the red food coloring. The green apple will show through the clear candy coating.

CARAMEL CORN

There was an old advertising campaign line that went, "Bet you can't eat just one!" That saying goes for this caramel corn as well as it did for the potato chips it helped sell. You'll know what I mean if you make this instead of regular popcorn the next time you rent a movie with friends. Trust me: if you have more than one oven, double or even triple this recipe, because your friends will eat as much as you can make.

3 quarts plain popped popcorn
(about ⅓ cup unpopped kernels)

6 tablespoons butter plus additional for
greasing the pan

1 cup light brown sugar

¼ cup light corn syrup

2 tablespoons hot water

1 teaspoon salt

½ teaspoon baking soda

1 tablespoon vanilla extract

1· Preheat the oven to 250°F. Butter an 11 × 17-inch baking pan or jelly-roll pan (preferably nonstick). Add the popped popcorn and set the pan aside.

2· Melt the 6 tablespoons butter in a heavy medium saucepan. Add the brown sugar, corn syrup, water, and salt. Stir over medium heat until the sugar dissolves completely and the syrup comes to a boil.

3· Clip a candy thermometer to the inside of the pan and cook, without stirring, until the mixture reaches 260°F (hard ball). Remove the pan from the heat and quickly stir in the baking soda and vanilla.

4· Pour the hot caramel over the popped popcorn and toss gently with 2 wooden spoons until all the popcorn is well coated. Bake in the preheated oven for 1 hour, stirring every 10 minutes. Remove the pan from the oven and place it on a cooling rack. Allow the caramel corn to cool completely in the pan. Store the caramel corn in an airtight container at room temperature for up to 2 weeks.

VARIATIONS

ALMOND CARAMEL CORN Reduce the amount of vanilla to 1 teaspoon. Add ½ teaspoon almond extract and 1 cup slivered almonds with the remaining vanilla and the baking soda.

COCONUT CARAMEL CORN Add 1 cup shredded, sweetened coconut with the vanilla and baking soda.

CRANBERRY CASHEW CARAMEL CORN Add ½ cup whole salted cashews and ½ cup whole dried cranberries with the vanilla and baking soda.

HAWAIIAN CARAMEL CORN Add ½ cup roughly chopped salted macadamia nuts and ½ cup roughly chopped dried pineapple with the vanilla and baking soda.

JACK'S PEANUT CARAMEL CORN Add 1 cup salted peanuts with the vanilla and baking soda.

RAISIN CARAMEL CORN Add 1 cup raisins (dark or golden) with the vanilla and baking soda.

RUM CARAMEL CORN Add 1 teaspoon artificial rum flavoring with the vanilla and baking soda.

CASHEW BRITTLE

The cans of golden cashews in the supermarket are usually roasted nuts. My recipe requires *raw* nuts, which are then roasted in the hot sugar syrup. Raw cashews are white and usually available in health food stores or in the produce section of gourmet markets. If you have trouble finding them, consult the Source Guide on page 242.

> 1¾ cups sugar
>
> ½ cup white corn syrup
>
> ¼ teaspoon salt
>
> ½ cup hot water
>
> 1½ heaping cups raw cashews
>
> 1 teaspoon butter plus additional for greasing the cookie sheet
>
> ½ teaspoon baking soda
>
> 1 teaspoon vanilla extract

1· Butter a large cookie sheet (preferably nonstick) and set it aside. Alternatively, butter a large marble slab. If you have a marble or granite counter, by all means use it. Simply clean it, then generously butter it.

2· Combine the sugar, corn syrup, salt, and water in a heavy large saucepan. Stir over medium heat until the sugar dissolves completely. Raise the heat to high and bring the mixture to a boil, without stirring.

3· Clip a candy thermometer onto the inside of the pan. Raise the heat to high and cook, without stirring, until the mixture reaches 290°F (just short of hard crack).

4· Remove the thermometer and stir in the nuts. Cook for 30 seconds more, stirring constantly. Remove the pan from the heat. Stir in the butter, baking soda, and vanilla. Be careful: the mixture will foam and rise.

5· When the foaming subsides, pour the hot candy onto the cookie sheet or the buttered marble slab. Pour it as thinly as possible, but do not spread the hot candy. After a few minutes, run a long, thin buttered spatula or knife under the candy to make sure it's not sticking.

6· While the candy is still quite warm, start pulling the brittle. Grab the edges, and stretch out the brittle. Pull it thin enough (about ¼ inch) to keep the nuts in one layer, if possible. Alternatively, use two buttered forks to help you pull and stretch the brittle.

7· As you pull, pieces of the brittle may break and holes may form. That's okay—you're going to break it into pieces later on anyway.

8· The brittle will become harder to pull as it cools, and will quickly become impossible to stretch without breaking. At this point, allow the brittle to cool completely, about 1 hour. Using your hands, break the brittle into small, irregular pieces about the size of a credit card. Store the brittle in an airtight container at room temperature for up to 1 month.

VARIATIONS

CASHEW BANANA BRITTLE Add ½ cup whole dried banana chips with the butter, baking soda, and vanilla.

CASHEW BLUEBERRY BRITTLE Add ½ cup whole dried blueberries with the butter, baking soda, and vanilla.

CASHEW CHERRY BRITTLE Add ½ cup whole dried cherries with the butter, baking soda, and vanilla.

CASHEW COCONUT BRITTLE Add ½ cup unsweetened coconut chips with the butter, baking soda, and vanilla.

CASHEW CRANBERRY BRITTLE Add ½ cup whole dried cranberries with the butter, baking soda, and vanilla.

CASHEW RAISIN BRITTLE Add ½ cup raisins (dark or golden) with the butter, baking soda, and vanilla.

CHICKPEA CANDY

MAKES ABOUT 1 POUND

I like to think of this candy as Middle Eastern brittle. It combines a distinctive Middle Eastern flavor, roasted chickpeas, with caramelized sugar. Roasted chickpeas make a great snack on their own and you can find them in many health food stores, Indian markets, or Middle Eastern specialty stores; or check the Source Guide on page 242.

1 cup sugar

½ cup light corn syrup

¼ cup water

1½ cups roasted chickpeas (do not use raw or canned chickpeas)

Butter or margarine for greasing the cookie sheet

1· Butter a large cookie sheet (preferably nonstick) and set it aside. Alternatively, butter a large marble slab. If you have a marble or granite counter, by all means use it. Simply clean it, then generously butter it.

2· Combine the sugar, corn syrup, and water in a heavy medium saucepan. Stir over medium heat until the sugar dissolves completely and the syrup comes to a boil.

3· Clip a candy thermometer to the inside of the pan. Raise the heat to high and cook, without stirring, until the mixture reaches 310°F (just over hard crack).

4· Immediately remove the pan from the heat. Remove the thermometer and stir in the chickpeas.

5· Pour the hot mixture as thinly as possible onto the prepared sheet or marble slab, but do not spread the hot candy. After a few minutes, run a long, thin buttered spatula or knife under the candy to make sure it's not sticking.

6· While the candy is still quite warm, start pulling the brittle. Grab the edges, and stretch out the candy. Pull it thin enough (about ¼ inch) to keep the chickpeas in one layer, if possible. Alternatively, use two buttered forks to help you pull and stretch the candy.

7· As you pull, pieces of the candy may break and holes may form. That's okay—you're going to break it into pieces later on anyway.

8· The candy will become harder to pull as it cools, and will quickly become impossible to stretch without breaking. At this point, allow the candy to cool completely, about 1 hour. Using your hands, break the candy into small, irregular pieces about the size of a credit card. Store the candy in an airtight container at room temperature for up to 1 month.

VARIATIONS

CUMIN CHICKPEA CANDY Add 1 teaspoon whole cumin seeds with the chickpeas.

HONEY CHICKPEA CANDY Reduce the corn syrup to ¼ cup. Add ⅓ cup honey with the remaining corn syrup.

SAFFRON CHICKPEA CANDY Omit the water from the recipe. Soak ½ teaspoon saffron threads in ¼ cup hot water for 15 minutes before starting the recipe. Add the saffron and the water to the pan with the sugar and corn syrup.

CHRISTMAS CANDY ORNAMENTS

The first year I made these and hung them on my tree, I made the mistake of adding flavoring to the candy. Save your money on flavoring, because these candy ornaments are not meant to be eaten! All through the holidays the lights of your tree make them sparkle. And at the end of the holidays, simply throw them away with your tree.

> 12 to 16 small cookie cutters (such as gingerbread men)
>
> 2½ cups sugar
>
> ¾ cup water
>
> ½ cup cream of tartar
>
> 4 to 6 drops food coloring as desired
>
> Vegetable oil for the cookie sheet

1· Oil a nonstick cookie sheet. Lightly oil the inside of the cookie cutters and place them on the cookie sheet and set it all aside. Alternatively, you can line a regular cookie sheet with parchment paper and lightly oil the parchment. Place the oiled molds on the parchment and set the sheet aside.

2· Combine the sugar, water, and cream of tartar in a heavy medium saucepan. Stir over medium heat until the sugar is dissolved and the mixture comes to a boil. Stir in the food coloring.

3· Clip a candy thermometer to the inside of the pan and cook the syrup, without stirring, until it reaches 300°F (hard crack). Remove the pan from the heat and allow the bubbling to subside.

4· Slowly pour enough syrup into each cookie cutter mold to cover the bottom, about ¼ inch thick. If your pan does not have a pouring spout, transferring the hot syrup to a Pyrex measuring cup with a handle and spout will make pouring the syrup into the molds easier.

5· While the candy is still hot, use the tip of a paring knife or the flat end of a bamboo skewer to make a small hole near the top of each ornament. If the candy has set to the point where you cannot push the knife through the sugar, you can always tie a ribbon around the entire ornament and hang it from your tree that way.

6· When the candy is still warm to the touch, remove the molds from the nonstick cookie sheet or peel them off the parchment. Gently push the candy ornaments out of the molds. They are fragile and unfortunately a few may shatter as you unmold them.

7· Thread a piece of ribbon through the hole you've created in the ornament or tie a ribbon around the whole shape to hang it on your tree.

VARIATION

DECORATED ORNAMENTS Although the clear-colored candy is beautiful on its own, you may want to add even more decoration to your candy ornaments. The easiest way is to gently drop pretty or unusual things onto the hot syrup just after pouring it into the molds.

Whatever you add will stick to the hot syrup and become part of the ornament. I've added candy flowers, Jordan almonds, crushed peppermint candies, rhinestone buttons, sparkles, gold and silver leaf, or small marbles.

There is no need to worry about using nonedible items such as buttons because these ornaments are not meant to be eaten. If you use things like buttons and want them back after the holidays, simply place your ornaments in a bowl of hot water and the sugar will dissolve, leaving your decorations behind.

COCONUT BRITTLE

This recipe requires unsweetened coconut, which is different from sweetened, shredded coconut. I have made it myself from fresh coconuts, but it is a lot of work. If you're up to the task, the recipe follows. If you prefer to buy unsweetened coconut, check your local health food or gourmet market; or consult the Source Guide on page 242.

> 1 cup sugar
> ½ cup light corn syrup
> ½ cup water
> 1 teaspoon unsalted butter plus additional
>   for greasing the cookie sheet
> ½ teaspoon salt
> 1½ cups shredded, unsweetened coconut
> 1 teaspoon vanilla extract
> ½ teaspoon baking soda

1· Butter a large cookie sheet (preferably nonstick) and set it aside. Alternatively, butter a large marble slab. If you have a marble or granite counter, by all means use it. Simply clean it, then generously butter it.

2· Combine the sugar, corn syrup, water, butter, and salt in a heavy 2½-quart saucepan. Stir over medium heat until the sugar dissolves completely and the syrup comes to a boil.

3· Clip a candy thermometer to the inside of the pan. Raise the heat to high and cook, without stirring, until the mixture reaches 240°F (soft ball).

4· Stir in the unsweetened coconut. Bring the mixture back to a boil and cook, stirring occasionally, until it reaches 290°F (just short of hard crack). Immediately remove the pan from the heat.

5· Stir in the vanilla and baking soda. Be careful: the mixture will foam and rise.

6· When the foaming subsides, pour the hot candy onto the cookie sheet or the buttered marble slab. Pour it as thinly as possible, but do not spread the hot candy. After a few minutes, run a long, thin buttered spatula or knife under the candy to make sure it's not sticking.

7· While the candy is still quite warm, start pulling the brittle. Grab the edges, and stretch out the brittle. Pull it thin enough (about ¼ inch) to keep the nuts in one layer, if possible. Alternately, use two buttered forks to help you pull and stretch the brittle.

8· As you pull, pieces of the brittle may break and holes may form. That's okay—you're going to break it into pieces later on anyway.

9· The brittle will become harder to pull as it cools, and will quickly become impossible to stretch without breaking. At this point, allow the brittle to cool completely, about 1 hour. Using your hands, break the brittle into small, irregular pieces about the size of a credit card. Store the brittle in an airtight container at room temperature for up to a month.

10· **TO MAKE UNSWEETENED SHREDDED COCONUT** Preheat the oven to 400°F.

11· Pierce two of the three eyes of a coconut with a clean screwdriver (or an oyster shucker). You may need to hit it with a hammer to drive it into the coconut.

12· Drain the liquid and place the coconut in the oven for 15 minutes or until the shell cracks. Allow the coconut to cool before proceeding.

13· Hit the coconut with a hammer to break it open. Pry the hard shell away from the coconut meat, using your tools if necessary. Use a vegetable peeler to take the brown skin off the white coconut meat.

14· Once you have all of the coconut meat removed and cleaned, grate it with a hand grater or a vegetable peeler, or break it into pieces and chop it finely in a food processor.

VARIATIONS

COCONUT BANANA BRITTLE Add ⅓ cup chopped dried bananas or banana chips with the vanilla and baking soda.

COCONUT BERRY BRITTLE Add ⅓ cup whole dried blueberries with the vanilla and baking soda.

COCONUT BRÛLÉ BRITTLE Allow the candy to reach 320°F before adding the vanilla and baking soda.

COCONUT RUM BRITTLE Add 1 teaspoon artificial rum flavoring with the vanilla and baking soda.

GLAZED SPICED WALNUTS

When served with before-dinner drinks, these nuts disappear in no time. They're appropriate for any occasion. I have made them for Superbowl parties as well as New Year's Eve extravaganzas.

> 2 teaspoons ground ancho chili powder
>
> 1 tablespoon superfine sugar
>
> ½ teaspoon salt
>
> 2 cups walnut halves
>
> 2 tablespoons water
>
> 1 teaspoon light brown sugar
>
> 1 tablespoon unsalted butter

1· Preheat the oven to 350°F.

2· Combine the chili powder, superfine sugar, and salt in a small bowl. Mix well and set aside.

3· Spread the walnuts on a cookie sheet and bake them for 5 to 7 minutes or until they're lightly toasted and fragrant.

4· Combine the water, brown sugar, and butter in a small saucepan. Cook over medium heat, stirring constantly, until the sugar is dissolved and the mixture comes to a boil. Add the nuts and stir until they are well coated. Continue cooking until all the liquid evaporates.

5· Pour the nuts into a large bowl and sprinkle with the sugar and spice mixture. Toss the nuts until they are well coated, then spread them on a cookie sheet to cool. Store the nuts in an airtight container at room temperature for up to 2 weeks.

VARIATIONS

GLAZED CURRIED ALMONDS Substitute 2 teaspoons curry powder for the ancho chili powder. Substitute 2 cups whole almonds for the walnuts.

GLAZED CURRIED CASHEWS Substitute 2 teaspoons curry powder for the ancho chili powder, and 2 cups raw cashews for the walnuts.

GLAZED SPICED PEANUTS Substitute 2 cups Spanish peanuts for the walnuts.

GLAZED SPICED PECANS Substitute 2 cups pecan halves for the walnuts.

GRANOLA CRISPY BARS

For extra crunch, these granola bars are baked twice, like biscotti. They are not very sweet and are actually good for you. They make a great gift for the athlete in your life.

1½ cups rolled oats

½ cup wheat germ

¼ cup slivered almonds

¼ cup chopped walnuts

¼ cup sunflower seeds

1 teaspoon ground cinnamon

¼ cup honey

¼ cup light brown sugar

¼ cup vegetable shortening, melted and cooled, plus additional for greasing the pan

2 teaspoons vanilla extract

2 large egg whites

¼ teaspoon salt

1· Preheat the oven to 350°F. Grease a 9 × 13-inch baking pan and set it aside.

2· Combine the oats, wheat germ, almonds, walnuts, sunflower seeds, and cinnamon in a large mixing bowl. Add the honey, brown sugar, shortening, and vanilla. Mix with a wooden spoon until all these ingredients are thoroughly combined.

3· In a medium mixing bowl, beat the egg whites and salt with an electric mixer on high, until soft peaks form. Fold the egg whites into the oat mixture until they are completely incorporated. Spread the mixture into the prepared pan and bake for 20 minutes.

4· Remove the pan from the oven and place it on a cooling rack for 10 minutes. Carefully cut the baked mixture into bars and lift them out of the pan with a spatula. Place the bars on an ungreased cookie sheet. Place them back in the oven and bake another 10 minutes or until they are dry and crisp.

5. Remove the cookie sheet from the oven and let the bars cool completely on a rack. Store them in an airtight container at room temperature for up to 3 weeks.

VARIATIONS

BUTTERSCOTCH RAISIN GRANOLA BARS Add ½ cup butterscotch chips with the beaten egg whites. Sure, the chips will melt and make the bars messier to cut and transfer from the pan to the cookie sheet; but it's worth it.

CHOCOLATE CHIP GRANOLA BARS Add ½ cup semisweet chocolate chips with the beaten egg whites. Sure, the chocolate will melt and make the bars messier to cut and transfer from the pan to the cookie sheet; but it's worth it.

CRANBERRY ORANGE GRANOLA BARS Substitute ⅓ cup whole dried cranberries for the sunflower seeds and add 2 teaspoons grated orange rind with the vanilla.

NUTTY RAISIN GRANOLA BARS Substitute ⅓ cup raisins (dark or golden) for the sunflower seeds.

TROPICAL GRANOLA BARS Omit the walnuts and sunflower seeds. Add ⅓ cup finely chopped macadamia nuts, ⅓ cup finely chopped dried pineapple, and ½ cup shredded sweetened coconut with the oats.

WHITE CHOCOLATE CHIP GRANOLA BARS Add ½ cup white chocolate chips with the beaten egg whites. Sure, the chocolate will melt and make the bars messier to cut and transfer from the pan to the cookie sheet; but it's worth it.

HAZELNUT BRITTLE

Like peanuts, hazelnuts have a natural seam down the middle, making them easy to split in half—and halved hazelnuts make a better brittle than whole ones. I use a sharp paring knife to split them apart. Raw hazelnuts come with a bitter skin attached which needs to be removed before you can use them in this recipe.

1½ cups unsalted raw hazelnuts, split in half

⅓ cup plus ½ teaspoon baking soda

⅓ cup water

¾ cup sugar

¾ cup light corn syrup

½ teaspoon salt

2 teaspoons butter plus additional for greasing the cookie sheet

2 teaspoons vanilla extract

1· Place the hazelnuts in a large saucepan and cover them with 5 cups water. Add ⅓ cup baking soda and stir until the baking soda dissolves. Place the pan over medium heat and bring the water to a boil. Boil the nuts for 3 minutes. Drain the nuts in a colander and rinse them in cold water. Remove the skins by rubbing the nuts together between your palms. Spread the nuts on paper towels to dry thoroughly before proceeding.

2· Butter a large cookie sheet (preferably nonstick) and set it aside. Alternatively, butter a large marble slab. If you have a marble or granite counter, by all means use it. Simply clean it, then generously butter it.

3· Combine the ⅓ cup water, the sugar, corn syrup, and salt in a heavy medium saucepan. Stir over medium heat until the sugar is completely dissolved and the syrup comes to a boil.

4· Clip a candy thermometer to the inside of the pan. Raise the heat to high and cook, without stirring, until the mixture reaches 240°F (soft ball). Stir in the nuts and bring the mixture back to a boil. Cook, stirring often, until the mixture reaches 310°F (just above hard crack).

5· Immediately remove the pan from heat. Stir in the butter, vanilla, and ½ teaspoon baking soda. Be careful: the mixture will foam and rise.

6· When the foaming subsides, pour the hot candy onto the cookie sheet or the buttered marble slab. Pour it as thinly as possible, but do not spread the hot candy. After a few minutes, run a long, thin buttered spatula or knife under the candy to make sure it's not sticking.

7· While the candy is still quite warm, start pulling the brittle. Grab the edges and stretch out the brittle. Pull it thin enough (about ¼ inch) to keep the nuts in one layer, if possible. Alternatively, use two buttered forks to help you pull and stretch the brittle.

8· As you pull, pieces of the brittle may break and holes may form. That's okay—you're going to break it into pieces later on anyway.

9· The brittle will become harder to pull as it cools, and will quickly become impossible to stretch without breaking. At this point, allow it to cool completely, about 1 hour. Using your hands, break the brittle into small, irregular pieces about the size of a credit card. Store the brittle in an airtight container at room temperature for up to 1 month.

VARIATIONS

HAZELNUT ALMOND BRITTLE Substitute ½ teaspoon almond extract for the vanilla.

HAZELNUT BLUEBERRY BRITTLE Add 1 cup whole dried blueberries with the butter, vanilla, and baking soda.

HAZELNUT BUTTER BRITTLE Increase the butter to ¼ cup.

HAZELNUT CINNAMON BRITTLE Add ¼ teaspoon ground cinnamon with the butter, vanilla, and baking soda.

HAZELNUT COFFEE BRITTLE Dissolve 1 tablespoon instant espresso powder in the ⅓ cup water before adding it to the pan.

LEMON DROPS

This classic hard candy is best made with hard-candy molds. Without molds, you can make small rounds on a cookie sheet lined with parchment paper. Citric acid is made from lemon juice and increases acidity, giving a delightfully sour taste to candy. Add too much and you'll guarantee lips will pucker. You can find citric acid in most gourmet shops and even some hardware stores that sell canning supplies.

⅛ teaspoon citric acid (optional, for a very sour taste)

1 cup sugar

⅓ cup corn syrup

½ cup water

1 teaspoon lemon extract or lemon oil

3 drops yellow food coloring (optional)

Vegetable oil for greasing the molds or cookie sheet

1· Lightly oil hard-candy molds and set them aside. Alternatively, oil a large cookie sheet and line it with parchment paper. Oil the parchment and set the sheet aside.

2· Dissolve the citric acid in 1 teaspoon water and combine it with the sugar, corn syrup, and water in a heavy medium saucepan. Stir over medium heat until the sugar is completely dissolved and the syrup comes to a boil.

3· Clip a candy thermometer to the inside of the pan and cook, without stirring, until the syrup reaches 300°F (hard crack).

4· Immediately remove the pan from the heat and allow the syrup to cool to 270°F. Stir in the lemon extract or oil and the food coloring, if using.

5· Pour the hot syrup into the prepared candy molds, following the manufacturer's instructions. Alternatively, pour teaspoonsful of the hot syrup onto the prepared cookie sheet, spacing them ½ inch apart. Transferring the hot syrup to a Pyrex measuring cup with a handle and a spout often makes shaping the candies much easier.

6· When the candies are completely cool, pop them out of the molds or peel them off the parchment. Wrap each piece of candy individually in wax paper or toss them all in powdered sugar. Store the candies in an airtight container at room temperature for up to 2 months.

VARIATIONS

CHERRY DROPS Substitute 1 teaspoon natural or artificial cherry flavoring for the lemon extract. Substitute red food coloring for the yellow food coloring.

HOREHOUND DROPS Omit the citric acid. Substitute 1 teaspoon horehound extract or flavoring for the lemon extract.

LICORICE DROPS Substitute 1 teaspoon natural or artificial anise flavoring for the lemon extract. Substitute black food coloring for the yellow food coloring.

ORANGE DROPS Substitute 1 teaspoon orange extract for the lemon extract. Substitute orange food coloring for the yellow food coloring.

LOLLIPOPS

You can make these timeless favorites with or without molds. Molds are available in endless shapes and styles. Check your local kitchenware store, or consult the Source Guide on page 242.

> 1 cup sugar
> ⅓ cup corn syrup
> ½ cup water
> ¼ teaspoon cream of tartar
> 1 teaspoon flavoring (see Note)
> 4 drops food coloring, optional
> 8 to 12 lollipop sticks
> Vegetable oil for greasing the cookie sheet
>   or molds

1· Oil a large cookie sheet and line it with parchment paper. Oil the parchment and set the sheet aside. Alternatively, prepare molds according to the manufacturer's instructions.

2· Combine the sugar, corn syrup, water, and cream of tartar in a heavy medium saucepan. Stir over medium heat until the sugar is completely dissolved and the syrup comes to a boil.

3· Clip a candy thermometer to the inside of the pan and cook, without stirring, until the syrup reaches 300°F (hard crack). Immediately remove the pan from the heat and allow the syrup to cool to 270°F. Stir in the flavoring and the food coloring.

4· Using half the syrup, pour 2-inch circles onto the prepared parchment, leaving at least 4 inches between each. Set the hot pan aside while you place the lollipop sticks—but work fast as the remaining syrup will cool quickly, becoming too thick to pour.

5· Create the lollipops by laying the sticks onto the sheet so that the tip of each stick lies at the center of its own circle.

6· Now pour the remaining syrup over the circles, thereby locking the sticks into the lollipop. During this second pouring, some of the syrup may spread out over the edges of the first circle, creating slightly larger lollipops.

7· Allow the lollipops to cool completely before peeling them off the parchment.

8· Alternatively, pour the hot syrup into molds following the manufacturer's instructions.

9· Wrap the lollipops individually in wax paper or small plastic lollipop bags. Store the candies at room temperature for up to 2 months.

NOTE ON FLAVORS Many flavors are commonly available in most supermarkets. Look for lemon extract, mint extract, artificial rum flavoring, natural or artificial coconut flavoring, rose water, natural or artificial banana flavoring, and more. You'll find them where you find spices and vanilla extract.

Specialty stores often carry natural flavorings like raspberry, strawberry, apple, caramel, clove, cinnamon, and more. For these and other unexpected artificial flavorings such as bubble gum, marshmallow, cheesecake, tutti-fruiti, saltwater taffy, grape, peanut butter, and eggnog, check the Source Guide on page 242.

You will also find that flavorings and molds often come with recipes, many of which call for as little as ¼ teaspoon of flavoring per batch. I find that 1 teaspoon gives the lollipops a powerful flavor right from the first lick.

VARIATIONS

CHRISTMAS LOLLIPOPS Use red or green food coloring. Use Christmas-shaped molds including Santas, angels, reindeer, snowmen, stockings, stars, or snowflakes.

DOUBLE-HITTER LOLLIPOPS Start with one flavor for the bottom circles. Use the entire batch of syrup and place the sticks into the circles as directed. Prepare a second batch of syrup in another color and flavor to cover the sticks. Possible combinations include banana/chocolate, coconut/pineapple, marshmallow/peanut butter, and lemon/cheesecake. The only limit is your imagination.

HERBAL LOLLIPOPS Although you can easily find natural liquid flavorings such as clove, cinnamon, and anise, you can make more exotic herbal lollipops, such as saffron, by steeping 1 teaspoon dried saffron in the ½ cup hot water for about ½ hour before making the lollipops. Do not strain the water before adding it to the pan. Other herbs such as basil, thyme, rosemary, and tarragon work as well. Use 2 tablespoons of chopped fresh herbs for these flavors and strain these herbs out before using the infused water.

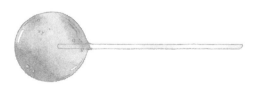

MACADAMIA NUT BRITTLE

Macadamia nuts are tropical nuts that are rich in oils. They are a Hawaiian specialty. Macadamia nuts are large, and need to be roughly chopped before using them in this brittle. If you have the patience, cut each one by hand into two or three pieces using a small paring knife. If you prefer, you can chop them with a large knife on a cutting board, but never chop them in the food processor or some of the nuts will pulverize, making the brittle cloudy.

½ cup water

1 cup sugar

¾ cup light corn syrup

1 heaping cup salted macadamia nuts, roughly chopped (about ⅓ pound)

1 teaspoon unsalted butter plus additional for greasing the cookie sheet

1 teaspoon vanilla extract

½ teaspoon baking soda

1· Butter a large cookie sheet (preferably nonstick) and set it aside. Alternatively, butter a large marble slab. If you have a marble or granite counter, by all means use it. Simply clean it, then generously butter it.

2· Combine the water, sugar, and corn syrup in a heavy medium saucepan. Stir over medium heat until the sugar is completely dissolved and the syrup comes to a boil.

3· Clip a candy thermometer into the inside of the pan. Raise the heat to high and cook, without stirring, until the mixture reaches 290°F (just short of hard crack). Stir in the nuts.

4· Bring the mixture back to a boil and cook, stirring often, until it reaches 300°F (hard crack).

5· Immediately remove the pan from the heat. Stir in the butter, vanilla, and baking soda. Be careful: the mixture will foam and rise.

6· When the foaming subsides, pour the hot candy onto the cookie sheet or the buttered marble slab. Pour it as thinly as possible, but do not spread the hot candy. After a few minutes, run a long, thin buttered spatula or knife under the candy to make sure it's not sticking.

7· While the candy is still quite warm, start pulling the brittle. Grab the edges, and stretch out the brittle. Pull it thin enough (about ¼ inch) to keep the nuts in one layer, if possible. Alternatively, use two buttered forks to help you pull and stretch the brittle.

8· As you pull, pieces of the brittle may break and holes may form. That's okay—you're going to break it into pieces later on anyway.

9· The brittle will become harder to pull as it cools, and will quickly become impossible to stretch without breaking. At this point, allow the brittle to cool completely, about 1 hour. Using your hands, break the brittle into small irregular pieces about the size of a credit card. Store the brittle in an airtight container at room temperature for up to a month.

VARIATIONS

MACADAMIA APRICOT BRITTLE Add ⅓ cup finely diced Australian glazed apricots with the butter, vanilla, and baking soda.

MACADAMIA COCONUT BRITTLE Add ¼ cup shredded unsweetened coconut chips to the syrup with the nuts.

MACADAMIA MANGO BRITTLE Add ⅓ cup finely diced dried mango with the butter, vanilla, and baking soda.

MACADAMIA PINEAPPLE BRITTLE Add ⅓ cup finely diced candied pineapple with the butter, vanilla, and baking soda.

NOUGATINE

Pastry chefs roll out this classic French almond brittle to create decorative touches to their desserts, or to make edible cups and plates. It can also be broken into pieces and simply enjoyed as a brittle.

> 2 cups sugar
> 2 cups slivered almonds, finely chopped
> Vegetable oil for greasing the foil

1· Wrap a cookie sheet in heavy-duty aluminum foil and generously oil the foil. Set it aside.

2· Place ⅔ cup sugar into a heavy medium saucepan and place the pan over medium heat. Stir until the sugar melts. Add another ⅔ cup sugar and stir until that sugar melts, too. Repeat with the final ⅔ cup sugar. Continue to cook the sugar until it is uniformly golden brown.

3· Immediately remove the pan from the heat and add the nuts all at once. Stir until the nuts are completely coated. Pour the mixture onto the oiled tray. Using an oiled metal spatula, spread the nougatine as thinly as possible. Allow the nougatine to cool completely, about 2 hours.

4· Peel the nougatine away from the foil and break it with your hands into irregular pieces, about the size of a credit card. Store the nougatine in an airtight container at room temperature for up to 1 month.

SERVING SUGGESTION: NOUGATINE BOWLS AND PLATES

Invert heatproof dessert bowls or 6- to 8-inch heatproof plates and cover them with heavy-duty foil. Generously oil the foil and place the covered bowls or plates on a cookie sheet covered with oiled foil. When the nougatine is cooked, ladle it over the inverted bowls or plates and spread it thin with an oiled spatula to completely cover the bowl or plate. When it's cool, peel the nougatine away from the foil to reveal edible candy tableware. Fill the bowls and plates with anything from ice cream to truffles. Makes about 8 small bowls or plates.

PEANUT BRITTLE

This is the old-fashioned peanut brittle I grew up on. I'd like to remember a Norman Rockwell childhood, but to be honest my mother never made candy. She did, however, buy us the finest candy she could find, usually at Bloomingdale's. As with many nut candies, the sweet and salty flavors make this version especially addictive.

1 cup sugar

½ cup light corn syrup

½ cup water

1 tablespoon butter plus additional for greasing the cookie sheet

1 teaspoon vanilla extract

1 teaspoon baking soda

1 cup salted roasted peanuts

1· Butter a large cookie sheet (preferably nonstick) and set it aside. Alternatively, butter a large marble slab. If you have a marble or granite counter, by all means use it. Simply clean it, then generously butter it.

2· Combine the sugar, corn syrup, and water in a heavy large saucepan. Stir over medium heat until the sugar is completely dissolved and the syrup comes to a boil.

3· Clip a candy thermometer to the inside of the pan. Raise the heat to high and cook, without stirring, until the mixture reaches 290°F (just short of hard crack).

4· Immediately remove the pan from the heat. Stir in the butter, vanilla, baking soda, and peanuts. Be careful: the mixture will foam and rise.

5· When the foaming subsides, pour the hot candy onto the cookie sheet or the buttered marble slab. Pour it as thinly as possible, but do not spread the hot candy. After a few minutes, run a long, thin buttered spatula or knife under the candy to make sure it's not sticking.

6· While the candy is still quite warm, start pulling the brittle. Grab the edges, and stretch out the brittle. Pull it thin enough (about ¼ inch) to keep the nuts in one layer, if possible. Alternatively, use two buttered forks to help you pull and stretch the brittle.

7· As you pull, pieces of the brittle may break and holes may form. That's okay—you're going to break it into pieces later on anyway.

8· The brittle will become harder to pull as it cools, and will quickly become impossible to stretch without breaking. At this point, allow the brittle to cool completely, about 1 hour. Using your hands, break the brittle into small, irregular pieces about the size of a credit card. Store the brittle in an airtight container at room temperature for up to 1 month.

VARIATIONS

BUTTERY PEANUT BRITTLE Increase the butter to ¼ cup.

GINGER PEANUT BRITTLE Add ¼ cup finely chopped candied ginger with the nuts.

MAPLE PEANUT BRITTLE Substitute 1 teaspoon artificial maple flavoring for the vanilla.

RUM PEANUT BRITTLE Substitute 1 teaspoon artificial rum flavoring for the vanilla.

PEANUT BUTTER FINGER CANDY

If you enjoy Butterfingers candy bars, this may become your favorite recipe in the book. While Butterfingers are always chocolate-covered, this candy bar doesn't need to be dipped in chocolate, unless you want to go the extra mile. I have served it both ways to great acclaim.

> 1 cup smooth peanut butter
> 1 teaspoon vanilla extract
> 1 cup sugar
> ⅓ cup light corn syrup
> ½ cup water
> Butter or margarine for greasing the pan

1· Butter a 9-inch square pan and set it aside.

2· Combine the peanut butter and vanilla in the top of a double boiler set over simmering water. If you don't have a double boiler, place the peanut butter and vanilla in a medium bowl that fits snugly over a pot of simmering water. Stir until the mixture is warm and well combined. Remove the top of the double boiler or the bowl from the simmering water. Cover the peanut butter to keep it warm and set it aside.

3· Combine the sugar, corn syrup, and water in a heavy medium saucepan. Place the pan over medium heat and stir until the sugar dissolves completely and the syrup comes to a boil.

4· Clip a candy thermometer to the inside of the pan. Raise the heat to high and continue to cook, without stirring, until the syrup reaches 290°F (just short of hard crack).

5· Remove the pan from the heat and remove the thermometer. Working quickly, stir in the warmed peanut butter. The mixture will thicken almost immediately. Quickly spread the mixture into the prepared 9-inch pan with a buttered spatula. Let the candy cool completely on a rack.

6· Turn the pan over and remove the candy in one piece. Use your hands to break it into irregular, bite-sized pieces. Store the candy in an airtight container at room temperature for up to 2 weeks.

VARIATIONS

BUTTERSCOTCH PEANUT BUTTER FINGER CANDY While it's still hot, spread ½ cup butterscotch chips on top of the candy. As the chips melt, use a 1-inch pastry brush to spread them over the top.

CHOCOLATE PEANUT BUTTER FINGER CANDY While it's still hot, spread ½ cup semisweet chocolate chips on top of the candy. As the chips melt, use a 1-inch pastry brush to spread them over the top.

DOUBLE CRUNCH PEANUT BUTTER FINGER CANDY Substitute 1 cup crunchy peanut butter for the smooth peanut butter.

WHITE CHOCOLATE PEANUT BUTTER FINGER CANDY While it's still hot, spread ½ cup white chocolate chips on top of the candy. As the chips melt, use a 1-inch pastry brush to spread them over the top.

PECAN BUTTER BRITTLE

I've put more butter in this brittle than any other brittle in the book. Butter just seems to go so well with pecans. This brittle is best made with pecan halves. Chopped pecans or pecan pieces can make the brittle cloudy.

¾ cup sugar

⅓ cup light corn syrup

⅓ cup water

⅛ teaspoon salt

¼ cup unsalted butter plus additional for greasing the cookie sheet

1 tablespoon vanilla extract

1 heaping cup pecan halves

1· Butter a large cookie sheet (preferably nonstick) and set it aside. Alternatively, butter a large marble slab. If you have a marble or granite counter, by all means use it. Simply clean it, then generously butter it.

2· Combine the sugar, corn syrup, water, and salt in a heavy medium saucepan. Stir over medium heat until the sugar dissolves completely and the syrup comes to a boil.

3· Clip a candy thermometer to the inside of the pan. Raise the heat to high and cook, without stirring, until the mixture reaches 290°F (just short of hard crack).

4· Immediately remove the pan from the heat and stir in the butter, vanilla, and nuts.

5· Pour the hot candy onto the cookie sheet or the buttered marble slab. Pour it as thinly as possible, but do not spread the hot candy. After a few minutes, run a long, thin buttered spatula or knife under the candy to make sure it's not sticking.

6· While the candy is still quite warm, start pulling the brittle. Grab the edges and stretch out the brittle. Pull it thin enough (about ¼ inch) to keep the nuts in one layer, if possible. Alternatively, use two buttered forks to help you pull and stretch the brittle.

7· As you pull, pieces of the brittle may break and holes may form. That's okay—you're going to break it into pieces later on anyway.

8· The brittle will become harder to pull as it cools, and will quickly become impossible to stretch without breaking. At this point, allow the brittle to cool completely, about 1 hour. Using your hands, break the brittle into small, irregular pieces about the size of a credit card. Store the brittle in an airtight container at room temperature for up to a month.

VARIATIONS

GINGER PECAN BUTTER BRITTLE Add ¼ cup finely chopped candied ginger with the nuts.

MAPLE PECAN BUTTER BRITTLE Add 1 teaspoon artificial maple flavoring with the nuts.

SPICED PECAN BUTTER BRITTLE Add 1 teaspoon crushed red pepper flakes with the nuts. Be careful: the hot syrup will bring out the chili oils. The fumes can be quite strong, so work in a well-ventilated kitchen.

TOFFEE PECAN BUTTER BRITTLE Increase the butter to ⅓ cup.

PISTACHIO BRITTLE

I won't buy pistachios until the day I plan to make this candy. Even if I buy 5 pounds more than I need, I will eat them all before I get to this brittle if they're in the house. Even cracking the shells becomes addictive. I always buy unsalted white nuts. The red nuts taste just the same, but the red dye will stain your fingers as you shell the nuts. If you can find shelled pistachios, buy them. They are more expensive but they will save you a lot of time.

⅓ cup water

¾ cup sugar

¾ cup light corn syrup

½ teaspoon salt

1¼ cups unsalted pistachio nuts

1 teaspoon butter plus additional for greasing the cookie sheet

½ teaspoon vanilla extract

½ teaspoon baking soda

1· Butter a large cookie sheet (preferably nonstick) and set it aside. Alternatively, butter a large marble slab. If you have a marble or granite counter, by all means use it. Simply clean it, then generously butter it.

2· Combine the water, sugar, corn syrup, and salt in a heavy medium saucepan. Place the pan over medium heat and stir until the sugar is completely dissolved and the syrup comes to a boil.

3· Clip a candy thermometer to the inside of the pan and cook, without stirring, until the syrup reaches 240°F (soft ball). Stir in the nuts.

4· Bring the mixture back to a boil and cook until it reaches 300°F (hard crack). Immediately remove the pan from the heat. Be careful not to overcook this brittle or the pistachios will burn.

5· Stir in the butter, vanilla, and baking soda. Be careful: the mixture will foam and rise.

6· When the foaming subsides, pour the hot candy onto the cookie sheet or the buttered marble slab. Pour it as thinly as possible, but do not spread the hot candy. After a few minutes, run a long, thin buttered spatula or knife under the candy to make sure it's not sticking.

7· While the candy is still quite warm, start pulling the brittle. Grab the edges, and stretch out the brittle. Pull it thin enough (about ¼ inch) to keep the nuts in one layer, if possible. Alternatively, use two buttered forks to help you pull and stretch the brittle.

8· As you pull, pieces of the brittle may break and holes may form. That's okay—you're going to break it into pieces later on anyway.

9· The brittle will become harder to pull as it cools, and will quickly become impossible to stretch without breaking. At this point, allow the brittle to cool completely, about 1 hour. Using your hands, break the brittle into small, irregular pieces about the size of a credit card. Store the brittle in an airtight container at room temperature for up to a month.

VARIATIONS

GREEN PISTACHIO BRITTLE Add the nuts when the temperature reaches 300°F. This will keep the nuts green and will not cook them as deeply.

PISTACHIO APRICOT BRITTLE Add ⅓ cup finely chopped dried apricots with the butter, vanilla, and baking soda.

PISTACHIO CARDAMOM BRITTLE Add 1 teaspoon whole cardamom seeds with the butter, vanilla, and baking soda.

PISTACHIO CINNAMON BRITTLE Add 1 teaspoon ground cinnamon with the butter, vanilla, and baking soda.

PISTACHIO HONEY BRITTLE Reduce the amount of the sugar to ¼ cup. Add ½ cup honey with the corn syrup.

PISTACHIO NUTMEG BRITTLE Add 1 teaspoon ground nutmeg with the butter, vanilla, and baking soda.

PUMPKIN SEED CRUNCH

MAKES ABOUT 1 ½ POUNDS

Pumpkin seeds, called pepitas in Mexican markets, are usually sold raw, shelled, and unsalted. You will need to toast them before making this recipe. It takes about 5 to 7 minutes in a skillet over medium heat. The seeds pop as they toast. When the popping stops, the seeds are done.

½ cup water

1 cup sugar

½ cup light corn syrup

1½ cups shelled, toasted pumpkin seeds (see above)

1 tablespoon butter plus additional for greasing the cookie sheet

1 tablespoon vanilla extract

½ teaspoon baking soda

1· Butter a large cookie sheet (preferably nonstick) and set it aside. Alternatively, butter a large marble slab. If you have a marble or granite counter, by all means use it. Simply clean it, then generously butter it.

2· Combine the water, sugar, and corn syrup in a heavy medium saucepan. Place the pan over medium heat and stir until the sugar is completely dissolved and the mixture comes to a boil.

3· Clip a candy thermometer to the inside of the pan and cook, without stirring, until the syrup reaches 285°F (just over soft crack). Stir in the toasted pumpkin seeds.

4· Bring the mixture back to a boil and cook, stirring often, until it reaches 300°F (hard crack). Immediately remove the pan from the heat.

5· Add the butter, vanilla, and baking soda. The mixture will be very thick and will foam.

6· When the foaming subsides, pour the hot candy onto the cookie sheet or the buttered marble slab. Pour it as thinly as possible, but do not spread the hot candy. After a few minutes, run a long, thin buttered spatula or knife under the candy to make sure it's not sticking.

7· While the candy is still quite warm, start pulling the candy. Grab the edges and stretch out the brittle. Pull it thin enough (about ¼ inch) to keep the nuts in one layer, if possible. Alternatively, use two buttered forks to help you pull and stretch the candy.

8· As you pull, pieces of the candy may break and holes may form. That's okay—you're going to break it into pieces later on anyway.

9· The candy will become harder to pull as it cools, and will quickly become impossible to stretch without breaking. At this point, allow the candy to cool completely, about 1 hour. Using your hands, break the candy into small, irregular pieces about the size of a credit card. Store the candy in an airtight container at room temperature for up to a month.

VARIATIONS

PUMPKIN HONEY CRUNCH Reduce the amount of sugar to ½ cup. Add ½ cup honey with the corn syrup.

PUMPKIN PIE CRUNCH Substitute ½ cup dark corn syrup for the light corn syrup. Stir in ½ teaspoon ground cinnamon just before adding the pumpkin seeds.

PUMPKIN SUNFLOWER CRUNCH Reduce the amount of toasted pumpkin seeds to 1 cup. Add ½ cup raw, unsalted, shelled sunflower seeds with the remaining pumpkin seeds.

TOFFEE PUMPKIN CRUNCH Increase the butter to ¼ cup.

SESAME CRUNCH

You can find this candy in almost every Chinese market. It sticks to your teeth and is totally satisfying. The flavor of the sesame seeds is deepened by the caramelized sugar. It can be cut into small, bite-sized pieces while still warm or broken into irregular shards once it has cooled.

> 5 tablespoons butter plus additional for
>   greasing the pan
> 1 cup sugar
> 1 cup white sesame seeds

1· Generously butter a 9 × 13-inch pan and set it aside.

2· Melt the 5 tablespoons butter over low heat in a heavy medium saucepan. Do not allow the butter to brown.

3· Add the sugar and raise the heat to medium. Stir constantly until the sugar dissolves and the syrup comes to a boil.

4· Clip a candy thermometer to the inside of the pan and cook, without stirring, until the syrup reaches 290°F (just short of hard crack).

5· Remove the thermometer. Stir in the sesame seeds and continue to cook, stirring often, until the candy turns dark amber. Immediately pour the hot candy into the prepared pan and spread as thinly as possible with a long buttered spatula.

6· Allow the candy to cool completely. Using your hands, break the candy into bite-sized pieces and store them in an airtight container at room temperature for up to 1 month.

VARIATIONS

BLACK SESAME SEED CRUNCH Substitute 1 cup black sesame seeds for the white sesame seeds.

FIVE-SPICE SESAME CRUNCH Add 1 teaspoon Chinese five-spice powder with the sesame seeds. See the Source Guide on page 242 for five-spice powder.

SOUTHERN PEANUT BRITTLE

Most peanuts are grown in the South. And this style of peanut brittle, which uses raw peanuts, became a favorite of southern peanut farmers' wives. Today it is often harder to find raw, shelled peanuts than roasted ones. You can always buy a large bag of peanuts in their shells and shell them yourself.

> 1 cup water
>
> 2 cups sugar
>
> ½ teaspoon salt
>
> 1 cup light corn syrup
>
> 2 cups raw unsalted peanuts
>
> 1 teaspoon unsalted butter plus additional
>   for greasing the cookie sheet
>
> ½ teaspoon baking soda

1· Butter a large cookie sheet (preferably nonstick) and set it aside. Alternatively, butter a large marble slab. If you have a marble or granite counter, by all means use it. Simply clean it, then generously butter it.

2· Combine the water, sugar, salt, and corn syrup in a heavy large saucepan. Stir over medium heat until the sugar is completely dissolved and the syrup comes to a boil.

3· Clip a candy thermometer to the inside of the pan. Raise the heat to high and cook, without stirring, until the mixture reaches 240°F (soft ball). Stir in the peanuts. Bring the mixture back to a boil and cook until it reaches 300°F (hard crack). Immediately remove the pan from the heat.

4· Stir in the butter and baking soda. Be careful: the mixture will foam and rise.

5· When the foaming subsides, pour the hot candy onto the cookie sheet or the buttered marble slab. Pour it as thinly as possible, but do not spread the hot candy. After a few minutes, run a long, thin buttered spatula or knife under the candy to make sure it's not sticking.

6· While the candy is still quite warm, start pulling the brittle. Grab the edges and stretch out the brittle. Pull it thin enough (about ¼ inch) to keep the nuts in one layer, if possible. Alternatively, use two buttered forks to help you pull and stretch the brittle.

7· As you pull, pieces of the brittle may break and holes may form. That's okay—you're going to break it into pieces later on anyway.

8· The brittle will become harder to pull as it cools, and will quickly become impossible to stretch without breaking. At this point, allow the brittle to cool completely, about 1 hour. Using your hands, break the brittle into small irregular pieces about the size of a credit card. Store the brittle in an airtight container at room temperature for up to a month.

VARIATIONS

GOLDEN RAISIN PEANUT BRITTLE Add ½ cup golden raisins with the butter and baking soda.

HOT MEXICAN PEANUT BRITTLE Add ½ teaspoon red chili pepper flakes with the butter and baking soda. Be careful: the hot syrup will bring out the chili oils. The fumes can be quite strong, so work in a well-ventilated kitchen.

SOUTHERN NUT AND HONEY BRITTLE Reduce the amount of the sugar to 1⅓ cups. Add ½ cup honey with the corn syrup.

SOUTHERN PEANUT PRALINE BRITTLE Increase the butter to 6 tablespoons.

SPONGE CANDY

Some old-time candy shops refer to this confection as *fairy food*. I prefer the name *sponge candy* because it resembles small pieces of broken sponge with all its tiny holes. The holes are formed when baking soda reacts with the vinegar, creating foam. Do not stir down the foam or you will lose all the tiny airholes. The unique flavor comes mostly from golden syrup, not to be confused with pancake, waffle, or even real maple syrup. Golden syrup is available in most supermarkets, wherever you find corn syrup and sugar.

> 1 cup golden syrup (see above)
> ½ cup sugar
> 1 teaspoon white vinegar
> 1 tablespoon baking soda
> Butter or margarine for greasing the pan

1· Butter a 10-inch square pan and line the bottom and sides with parchment paper. Butter the parchment and set the pan aside.

2· Combine the golden syrup, sugar, and vinegar in a large heavy pan and stir over medium heat until the sugar is completely dissolved and the mixture comes to a boil.

3· Clip a candy thermometer to the inside of the pan. Cook, without stirring, until the mixture reaches 300°F (hard crack). Immediately remove the pan from the heat.

4· Stir in the baking soda. Be careful: the mixture will foam and rise. Pour the foaming syrup immediately into the prepared 10-inch pan. Do not spread the mixture, as the foam will give the candy its spongy look.

5· Allow the candy to cool completely. Slip the end of a flexible spatula under the edge of the candy and remove the candy from the pan in one piece, if possible. Use the dull side of a heavy knife or cleaver to break the candy into bite-sized pieces. Wrap each piece individually in wax paper and store them in an airtight container at room temperature for up to 1 week.

VARIATIONS

MAPLE SPONGE CANDY Reduce the amount of golden syrup to ½ cup. Add ½ cup maple syrup with the vinegar.

MILK CHOCOLATE SPONGE CANDY Dip the pieces of cooled sponge candy into melted milk chocolate (for advice on melting chocolate, see page 11). Lay the pieces of dipped candy on wax paper and refrigerate them until they are set.

SEMISWEET CHOCOLATE SPONGE CANDY Dip the pieces of cooled sponge candy into melted semisweet chocolate (for advice on melting chocolate, see page 11). Lay the pieces of dipped candy on wax paper and refrigerate them until they are set.

WHITE CHOCOLATE SPONGE CANDY Dip the pieces of cooled sponge candy into melted white chocolate (for advice on melting chocolate, see page 11). Lay the pieces of dipped candy on wax paper and refrigerate them until they are set.

TOFFEE

This English treat is sometimes called butter crunch. It's the filling for Heath bars. Now you can make this buttery, crunchy filling on your own. Because butter is the main flavoring ingredient, use the best you can find. Many specialty markets sell French and English butter, which will give your candy an authentic European taste.

> 1½ cups unsalted butter (3 sticks) plus
>   additional for greasing the pan
>
> 2 cups sugar
>
> ¼ cup water
>
> 3 tablespoon light corn syrup

1 · Butter a jelly-roll pan or an 11 × 17-inch baking pan. Place it on a cooling rack and set it aside.

2 · Melt the butter in a heavy large saucepan over medium heat. Do not allow the butter to brown. Add the sugar, water, and corn syrup to the melted butter. Stir until the sugar is completely dissolved. Bring the mixture to a boil without stirring.

3 · Clip a candy thermometer to the inside of the pan. Continue to cook, without stirring, until the mixture reaches 300°F (hard crack).

4 · Remove the pan from the heat and immediately pour the hot syrup into the prepared jelly-roll pan or 11 × 17-inch baking pan. The syrup will spread thin but may not reach the corners of the pan. Do not spread it any farther.

5 · Allow the candy to cool completely in the pan. Slip the end of a flexible spatula under the edge of the candy and lift the candy up in one piece. Use your hands to break it into bite-sized, irregular pieces. Store the candy in an airtight container at room temperature for up to 2 weeks.

VARIATIONS

ALMOND TOFFEE Add 1½ cups slivered almonds to the pan when the syrup reaches 290°F. Continue to cook, stirring often, until it reaches 300°F.

BUTTERSCOTCH TOFFEE While it's still hot, spread ½ cup butterscotch chips on top of the candy. As the chips melt, use a 1-inch pastry brush to spread them over the top.

MILK CHOCOLATE TOFFEE While it's still hot, spread ½ cup milk chocolate chips on top of the candy. As the chips melt, use a 1-inch pastry brush to spread them over the top.

SEMISWEET CHOCOLATE TOFFEE While it's still hot, spread ½ cup semisweet chocolate chips on top of the candy. As the chips melt, use a 1-inch pastry brush to spread them over the top.

WHITE CHOCOLATE TOFFEE While it's still hot, spread ½ cup white chocolate chips on top of the candy. As the chips melt, use a 1-inch pastry brush to spread them over the top.

S O U R C E   G U I D E

IF YOU CAN'T FIND a particular ingredient or a piece of equipment, these specialty shops can send you what you need to make the recipes in this book. Many also have Web sites for easy ordering.

KALUSTYAN'S

123 Lexington Ave.
New York, NY 10016
1-212-685-3451
www.kalustyans.com
A large selection of herbs, spices, nuts, fruits, coconut, and natural flavorings from around the world.

KITCHEN KRAFTS

P.O. Box 442
Waukon, IA 52172-0442
1-800-776-0575
www.kitchenkrafts.com
The complete source for candy-making supplies. Molds are available in every shape and size for hard candy, chocolate, jelly candy, caramels, and more, along with hard-to-find ingredients and

equipment. If you're not sure what you need, the helpful staff will be more than happy to make suggestions.

KITCHEN MARKET

218 Eighth Ave.
New York, NY 10011
1-888-HOT-4433
Dried fruits and nuts of all kinds, including unsweetened coconut, as well as chocolate and spices.

LORRAINE

148 Broadway
Hanover, MA 02339
1-617-826-2877
Candy molds, chocolate, lollipop bags, thermometers, food colorings, and more.

NEW YORK CAKE AND BAKING DISTRIBUTORS

56 West 22nd St.
New York, NY 10010
1-212-675-CAKE
1-800-942-2539
All the baking and candy-making supplies
you can imagine, including a full range of
artificial and natural flavorings, lollipop
sticks, molds, and candy thermometers.
They also carry chocolate in bulk and 1-
pound bags, as well as almond paste,
glycerin, gold and silver leaf, gold and
silver dust, and candy colorings. They
carry marble slabs and nonstick cookie
sheets in many sizes, as well as nonstick
Silpat sheets in small and large sizes to fit
any cookie sheet.

SWEET CELEBRATIONS

7009 Washington Ave. South
Edina, MN 55439
1-800-328-6722
Name a type of chocolate and they'll have
it—along with flavorings, food colorings,
molds, lollipop sticks, lollipop bags, and
candy or chocolate thermometers.

SWEET CREATIONS

588 W800 S.
Bountiful, UT 84010-8106
1-800-289-9950
www.lollipopmolds.com
Lollipop molds in many shapes and sizes
with flavorings, sticks, bags,
thermometers, and candy decorations.
Their Web site has pictures on how to use
their molds.

VERVE

305 Dudley St.
Providence, RI 02907
1-401-351-6415
Gum base in bulk and 2-ounce packages.

INDEX